Labour Law

\

Chapter 1

Introduction

1.1 Introduction

India has embarked on an ambitious legal reform journey with the enactment of three groundbreaking codes: the Bharatiya Nyay Sanhita, 2023 (Indian Civil Code), the Bharatiya Nagarik Suraksha Sanhita, 2023 (Indian Code of Civil Protection), and the Bharatiya Sakshya, 2023 (Indian Evidence Code). These comprehensive legislations have the potential to reshape the Indian legal landscape, ushering in a new era of clarity, efficiency, and modernization across various domains of civil laws, civil protection measures, and evidentiary rules.

1.2 The Bharatiya Nyay Sanhita, 2023: A Transformative Civil Code

The Bharatiya Nyay Sanhita, 2023, is a landmark legislation that consolidates and codifies the civil laws of India into a single, coherent framework. This monumental task, undertaken after decades of deliberation and consultation, aims to simplify and harmonize the complex web of civil laws that have evolved over time.

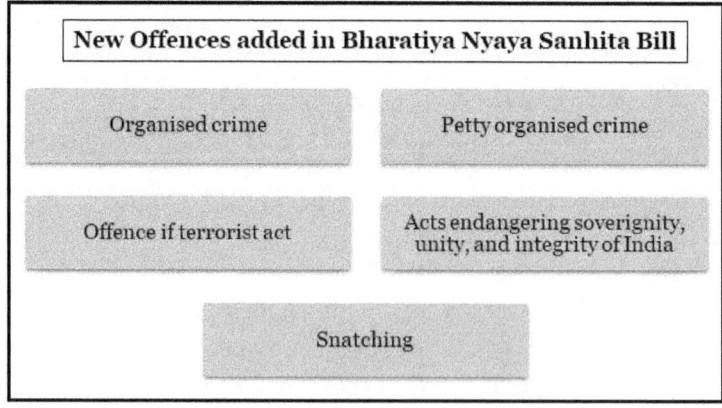

Prior to the enactment of this code, India's civil laws were primarily derived from a combination of statutory laws, case laws, and customary practices, often leading to inconsistencies, ambiguities, and overlapping jurisdictions. The Bharatiya Nyaya Sanhita, 2023, seeks to address these challenges by providing a comprehensive and unified legal framework for civil matters.

The code encompasses a wide range of civil matters, including contracts, property rights, torts, family disputes, and various other areas of civil jurisprudence. It draws upon the best practices and principles from existing laws, while also incorporating contemporary legal developments and societal needs.

One of the key objectives of the Bharatiya Nyaya Sanhita, 2023, is to enhance clarity and accessibility for all stakeholders, including lawyers, judges, businesses, and the general public. By consolidating and codifying the civil laws, the code aims to reduce the complexity and uncertainty that often arise from interpreting multiple sources of law.

Additionally, the code seeks to promote uniformity and consistency in the application of civil laws across different jurisdictions within India. This is particularly important in a diverse and federal nation like India, where variations in legal interpretations and practices can lead to disparities and inequalities.

The Bharatiya Nagarik Suraksha Sanhita, 2023: Safeguarding Civil Protection

In an increasingly complex and interconnected world, the need for comprehensive and robust civil protection measures has become paramount. The Bharatiya Nagarik Suraksha Sanhita, 2023, is a pioneering effort to establish a comprehensive framework for civil protection in India.

This code addresses a wide range of issues related to public safety, disaster management, emergency response, and citizen welfare. It aims to enhance the resilience of communities and ensure effective preparedness and response mechanisms in the face of natural or man-made calamities.

The Bharatiya Nagarik Suraksha Sanhita, 2023, encompasses various aspects of civil protection, including:

1. Disaster Risk Reduction: The code outlines strategies and measures for reducing the risk of disasters through proactive planning, risk assessment, and mitigation efforts.

2. Emergency Management: It establishes a robust framework for emergency management, including early warning systems, emergency response protocols, and coordination mechanisms between various stakeholders.

3. Critical Infrastructure Protection: The code addresses the protection of critical infrastructure, such as power grids, communication networks, and transportation systems, which are essential for the functioning of modern societies.

4. Public Safety and Security: It encompasses provisions related to public safety, including law enforcement, crowd management, and measures to prevent and respond to acts of terrorism or civil unrest.

5. Humanitarian Assistance and Relief: The code provides guidelines for the effective delivery of humanitarian assistance and relief efforts in the aftermath of disasters or emergencies, ensuring coordinated and efficient aid distribution.

6. Citizen Welfare and Resilience: It emphasizes the importance of building resilient communities by promoting awareness, education, and capacity-building programs for citizens, enabling them to better prepare for and respond to emergencies.

The Bharatiya Nagarik Suraksha Sanhita, 2023, recognizes the critical role of effective coordination and collaboration among various stakeholders, including government agencies, non-governmental organizations, private sector entities, and local communities. It establishes mechanisms for seamless communication, resource sharing, and joint decision-making processes to enhance the effectiveness of civil protection measures.

1.2.1 Modernizing Evidentiary Rules

The Bharatiya Sakshya, 2023, is a significant reform in the realm of evidentiary laws in India. This code consolidates and modernizes the rules governing the admissibility, relevance, and weight of evidence in legal proceedings, ensuring fairness, transparency, and alignment with international best practices.

Prior to the enactment of this code, India's evidentiary laws were primarily governed by the Indian Evidence Act of 1872, which, despite numerous amendments over the years, had become outdated and inadequate to address the complexities of modern legal proceedings.

The Bharatiya Sakshya, 2023, seeks to address these limitations by introducing a comprehensive and forward-looking framework for evidentiary rules. It draws upon contemporary legal principles, technological advancements, and evolving societal norms to ensure that the evidentiary process is efficient, fair, and aligned with the principles of justice.

One of the key objectives of the Bharatiya Sakshya, 2023, is to streamline the evidentiary process and reduce the time and resources spent on procedural matters. It achieves this by clearly defining the rules for admissibility of evidence, establishing guidelines for the evaluation of different types of evidence, and providing mechanisms for the efficient handling of evidentiary disputes.

The code also addresses the challenges posed by technological advancements and the increasing reliance on digital evidence. It establishes clear guidelines for the admissibility and authentication of electronic evidence, ensuring that legal proceedings can effectively handle modern forms of evidence while maintaining the integrity of the evidentiary process.

Furthermore, the Bharatiya Sakshya, 2023, recognizes the importance of protecting the rights of individuals and ensuring fair trials. It incorporates provisions related to the exclusion of illegally obtained evidence, the protection of privileged communication, and the rights of witnesses and victims, among other safeguards.

1.2.2 The Impact on Labour Laws

The enactment of the Bharatiya Nyay Sanhita, 2023, the Bharatiya Nagarik Suraksha Sanhita, 2023, and the Bharatiya Sakshya, 2023, has far-reaching implications that extend beyond the realms of civil laws, civil protection, and evidentiary rules. These new codes are bound to have a profound impact on various sectors, including the realm of labor laws, which play a crucial role in shaping the rights and welfare of workers, the obligations of employers, and the overall economic and social landscape of the country.

Labour laws in India have a rich and evolving history, rooted in the principles of social justice, worker protection, and industrial harmony. The origins of labour legislation in India can be traced back to the colonial era, when the first labour laws were introduced to regulate working conditions in factories and plantations. Post-independence, India witnessed a surge in labour legislation, with the enactment of various acts and regulations aimed at safeguarding the rights and welfare of workers. Some of the key labour laws currently in force in India include:

1. The Industrial Disputes Act, 1947: This act governs the resolution of industrial disputes, provides mechanisms for conciliation and adjudication, and regulates strikes and lockouts.

2. The Minimum Wages Act, 1948: This act ensures the payment of minimum wages to workers, with the aim of preventing exploitation and ensuring a basic standard of living.

3. The Contract Labour (Regulation and Abolition) Act, 1970: This act regulates the employment of contract labour and aims to abolish the practice of contract labour in certain industries and occupations.

4. The Equal Remuneration Act, 1976: This act prohibits discrimination in the payment of remuneration on the basis of gender and promotes equal pay for equal work.

5. The Employees' Provident Funds and Miscellaneous Provisions Act, 1952: This act establishes a provident fund scheme for employees in certain establishments, providing social security benefits and retirement savings.

6. The Employees' State Insurance Act, 1948: This act provides for certain benefits to employees in case of sickness, maternity, and employment-related injuries or disabilities.

7. The Payment of Gratuity Act, 1972: This act mandates the payment of gratuity, a lump-sum amount, to employees upon retirement or termination of employment, subject to certain conditions.

8. The Maternity Benefit Act, 1961: This act regulates the employment of women in certain establishments and provides for maternity benefits and other related facilities.

9. The Child Labour (Prohibition and Regulation) Act, 1986: This act prohibits the employment of children below a certain age in hazardous occupations and regulates their employment in non-hazardous occupations.

10. The Building and Other Construction Workers (Regulation of Employment and Conditions of Service) Act, 1996: This act regulates the employment and conditions of service of construction workers and provides for their safety, health, and welfare measures.

Despite the comprehensive nature of these labour laws, there has been a growing need for reform and consolidation. The existing labour laws are often criticized for being complex, outdated, and fragmented, leading to compliance challenges for employers and hampering the ease of doing business. Moreover, the rapid changes in the global economic landscape, technological advancements, and evolving work patterns have necessitated a review and modernization of labour laws to ensure their relevance and effectiveness.

The rationale behind the introduction of the new codes, such as the Bharatiya Nyaya Sanhita, 2023, the Bharatiya Nagarik Suraksha Sanhita, 2023, and the Bharatiya Sakshya, 2023, stems from the need to simplify and harmonize the legal framework, enhance transparency, promote economic growth, and align with international best practices, while maintaining worker protection and social welfare.

The introduction of the comprehensive legal reforms through the Bharatiya Nyay Sanhita, 2023 (Indian Code of Laws), the Bharatiya Sakshya, 2023 (Indian Evidence Act), and the Bharatiya Nagarik Suraksha Sanhita, 2023 (Indian Civil Protection Code), is expected to have a profound and multidimensional impact on the labour laws and their implementation in India. These landmark legislations, aimed at modernizing and consolidating various areas of law, will inevitably intersect with the realm of labour and employment, leading to a seismic shift in the legal landscape governing the world of work.

1.3 Contract Law and Employment Agreements:

The Bharatiya Nyay Sanhita, 2023, through its comprehensive overhaul of contract law, is poised to reshape the very foundation upon which employment relationships are built. This code, by introducing a harmonized and modernized framework for contracts, will undoubtedly influence the interpretation, negotiation, and enforcement of employment agreements across various sectors.

One area likely to be impacted is the realm of non-compete clauses, which are often incorporated into employment contracts to protect an employer's trade secrets and prevent employees from joining or establishing competing businesses. The Bharatiya Nyaya Sanhita, 2023, may provide clearer guidelines on the enforceability of such clauses, striking a balance between an employer's legitimate interests and an employee's right to pursue gainful employment.

Severance agreements, which outline the terms and conditions governing the termination of employment, may also be subject to scrutiny under the new contract law provisions. The code may establish parameters for fair and equitable severance packages, addressing issues such as notice periods, compensation calculations, and the waiver of legal claims.

Furthermore, the Bharatiya Nyaya Sanhita, 2023, is expected to introduce streamlined and efficient dispute resolution mechanisms, which could have a profound impact on the adjudication of employment-related disputes. This may include provisions for mediation, arbitration, or specialized tribunals to resolve conflicts arising from employment agreements, potentially reducing the burden on traditional court systems and expediting the resolution process.

1.3.1 Property Rights and Workplace Safety:

The Bharatiya Nyaya Sanhita, 2023, by virtue of its comprehensive treatment of property rights and tort law, is likely to influence the application of labour laws related to workplace safety, liability for workplace accidents, and compensation mechanisms for occupational injuries or diseases.

Under the current legal framework, workplace safety is primarily governed by the Factories Act, 1948, the Mines Act, 1952, and various other sector-specific regulations. However, the Bharatiya Nyaya Sanhita, 2023, may introduce overarching principles and legal doctrines that could reshape the interpretation and implementation of these existing labour laws.

For instance, the code's provisions on property rights and the duty of care owed by property owners could potentially extend to employers and their obligations towards ensuring a safe and secure working environment for their employees. This could lead to heightened scrutiny of workplace conditions, safety protocols, and the adequacy of protective measures implemented by employers.

Moreover, the tort law provisions of the Bharatiya Nyaya Sanhita, 2023, may impact the legal remedies available to workers who suffer injuries or occupational diseases due to negligence or breach of duty by their employers. The code may clarify the standards of liability, causation, and the quantification of damages in such cases, potentially influencing the compensation mechanisms and legal recourse available to affected workers.

1.3.2 Family Laws and Maternity Benefits:

The family law provisions enshrined in the Bharatiya Nyaya Sanhita, 2023, are expected to have ripple effects on labour laws related to maternity benefits, paternity leave, and other family-related provisions for employees.

Currently, the Maternity Benefit Act, 1961, governs various aspects of maternity leave, medical benefits, and job protection for women employees during pregnancy and childbirth. However, the Bharatiya Nyaya Sanhita, 2023, by establishing a comprehensive framework for family law, may necessitate a review and alignment of these existing labour laws to ensure consistency and coherence.

The code's provisions on parental rights, adoption, and surrogacy arrangements may prompt employers and policymakers to re-evaluate the scope and applicability of maternity and parental leave policies. For instance, the recognition of diverse family structures and alternative parenthood arrangements under the new code could pave the way for more inclusive and equitable leave policies, catering to the needs of different family configurations.

Additionally, the Bharatiya Nyaya Sanhita, 2023, may influence the implementation of workplace policies related to childcare facilities, flexible work arrangements, and other family-friendly measures designed to support working parents. By establishing guiding principles and legal frameworks for family obligations, the code may catalyze a shift towards more comprehensive and progressive labour laws in this domain.

1.3.3 Civil Disputes and Industrial Disputes Resolution:

The mechanisms for dispute resolution and the evidentiary rules established by the Bharatiya Nyaya Sanhita, 2023, and the Bharatiya Sakshya, 2023, respectively, are poised to have a significant impact on the adjudication of industrial disputes, grievance redressal processes, and the admissibility and evaluation of evidence in labour-related cases.

The Industrial Disputes Act, 1947, currently governs the resolution of industrial disputes, including provisions for conciliation, adjudication, and enforcement of awards. However, the Bharatiya Nyaya Sanhita, 2023, by introducing a comprehensive and streamlined dispute resolution framework, may necessitate a review and harmonization of these existing labour laws.

The code's provisions on alternative dispute resolution mechanisms, such as mediation and arbitration, could be extended to the realm of industrial disputes, potentially offering more efficient and cost-effective means of resolving labour-related conflicts. This could reduce the burden on traditional adjudicatory bodies and promote timely resolution of disputes, minimizing disruptions to industrial operations.

Furthermore, the Bharatiya Sakshya, 2023, by overhauling the rules of evidence, may influence the admissibility and evaluation of various forms of evidence in labour-related legal proceedings. This could include the treatment of electronic records, surveillance footage, witness testimonies, and expert opinions, all of which play a crucial role in substantiating claims and resolving disputes in the labour context.

1.3.4 Emergency Preparedness and Worker Safety:

The Bharatiya Nagarik Suraksha Sanhita, 2023 (Indian Civil Protection Code), by establishing a robust framework for civil protection and emergency management, is poised to have significant implications for labour laws related to worker safety, emergency response protocols, and workplace disaster preparedness measures.

Existing labour laws, such as the Factories Act, 1948, and the Mines Act, 1952, already mandate certain safety measures and emergency response protocols for industrial establishments. However, the Bharatiya Nagarik Suraksha Sanhita, 2023, by introducing a comprehensive and unified approach to civil protection, may necessitate a review and alignment of these sector-specific labour laws.

The code's provisions on emergency planning, disaster risk reduction, and crisis management could influence the development of workplace-specific emergency preparedness plans, evacuation procedures, and employee training programs. Employers may be required to adopt more robust and coordinated measures to ensure the safety and well-being of their workforce in the event of natural disasters, industrial accidents, or other emergencies.

Furthermore, the Bharatiya Nagarik Suraksha Sanhita, 2023, may provide guidance on the roles and responsibilities of employers, employees, and relevant authorities during emergency situations, clarifying the obligations and liabilities associated with worker safety and emergency response.

1.4 Critical Infrastructure Protection and Essential Services:

The provisions of the Bharatiya Nagarik Suraksha Sanhita, 2023, regarding critical infrastructure protection, are likely to have a significant impact on labour laws governing essential services, strike regulations, and the rights and obligations of workers in sectors deemed critical for public safety and national security.

Existing labour laws, such as the Essential Services Maintenance Act (ESMA), already regulate strikes and work stoppages in certain essential services, such as healthcare, transportation, and utilities. However, the Bharatiya Nagarik Suraksha Sanhita, 2023, by introducing a comprehensive framework for identifying and protecting critical infrastructure, may necessitate a review and realignment of these existing labour laws.

The code's provisions on critical infrastructure protection could potentially expand or redefine the scope of essential services, leading to modifications in strike regulations and the rights of workers in these sectors. This may involve striking a delicate balance between the fundamental right to strike and the need to ensure the uninterrupted provision of services deemed essential for public safety and national security.

Furthermore, the Bharatiya Nagarik Suraksha Sanhita, 2023, may introduce specific measures and protocols for ensuring the continuity of operations and the protection of critical infrastructure during emergencies or industrial disputes. This could include provisions for contingency planning, emergency staffing, and the deployment of specialized personnel to maintain essential services.

1.5 Evidentiary Rules in Labour Disputes:

The Bharatiya Sakshya, 2023 (Indian Evidence Act), by modernizing the rules of evidence, is poised to impact the admissibility and evaluation of various forms of evidence in labour-related legal proceedings. This could have far-reaching implications for the adjudication of labour disputes, grievances, and other employment-related matters.

Currently, the Indian Evidence Act, 1872, governs the admissibility and evaluation of evidence in legal proceedings, including those related to labour disputes. However, the Bharatiya Sakshya, 2023, by introducing a comprehensive overhaul of evidentiary rules, may necessitate a review and alignment of the existing legal framework governing labour disputes.

One area likely to be impacted is the treatment of electronic records and digital evidence, which have become increasingly prevalent in the modern workplace. The Bharatiya Sakshya, 2023, may establish clear guidelines on the admissibility, authentication, and evidentiary weight accorded to electronic communications, surveillance footage, digital logs, and other forms of electronic evidence in labour-related cases.

Furthermore, the code's provisions on witness testimony and expert opinions could influence the evaluation of evidence in labour disputes. This may include guidelines on the credibility of witness statements, the admissibility of expert opinions on matters such as workplace conditions or occupational health, and the weight accorded to such evidence in legal proceedings.

The modernization of evidentiary rules under the Bharatiya Sakshya, 2023, could also facilitate the adoption of technology-assisted evidence gathering and presentation in labour-related cases, potentially streamlining the litigation process and enhancing the accuracy and efficiency of evidence evaluation.

1.6 Rights and Protections for Vulnerable Workers:

The principles of fairness, non-discrimination, and social justice embedded in the new codes are expected to influence labour laws aimed at protecting the rights and welfare of vulnerable workers, such as migrant workers, informal sector workers, or workers with disabilities.

Existing labour laws, such as the Interstate Migrant Workmen Act, 1979, and the Unorganized Workers' Social Security Act, 2008, already provide certain protections and benefits for vulnerable segments of the workforce. However, the overarching principles enshrined in the Bharatiya Nyaya Sanhita, 2023, and the Bharatiya Nagarik Suraksha Sanhita, 2023, may necessitate a review and strengthening of these existing labour laws.

The Bharatiya Nyaya Sanhita, 2023, by emphasizing principles of non-discrimination and equal treatment, could influence labour laws pertaining to the recruitment, employment conditions, and termination processes for vulnerable workers. This may include provisions prohibiting discriminatory practices based on factors such as gender, disability, or migratory status, and ensuring equal access to employment opportunities and fair working conditions.

Furthermore, the Bharatiya Nagarik Suraksha Sanhita, 2023, by underscoring the importance of social security and welfare, could pave the way for enhanced protections and benefits for vulnerable workers. This could include measures such as mandatory health insurance, access to social security schemes, and provisions for safe and secure housing and living conditions for migrant workers or those employed in the informal sector.

1.7 Alignment with International Labour Standards:

The introduction of the new codes presents an opportunity to review and align Indian labour laws with international labour standards and conventions, promoting harmonization and facilitating cross-border trade and investment.

India has ratified several international labour conventions and treaties, such as those promulgated by the International Labour Organization (ILO). However, the existing labour laws in India may not fully comply with or reflect the principles and standards enshrined in these international instruments.

The Bharatiya Nyay Sanhita, 2023, and the Bharatiya Nagarik Suraksha Sanhita, 2023, by establishing comprehensive and modern legal frameworks, provide an opportune moment to assess the alignment of Indian labour laws with international standards. This could involve reviewing provisions related to freedom of association, collective bargaining rights, prohibition of forced labour, abolition of child labour, and non-discrimination in employment, among others.

By aligning Indian labour laws with international standards, the new codes could facilitate greater integration with the global economy, attract foreign investment, and enhance India's reputation as a responsible and compliant member of the international community. This alignment could also promote the protection of workers' rights, decent working conditions, and the promotion of social dialogue and tripartism in labour relations.

1.8 Compliance and Enforcement:

The streamlining and consolidation of laws under the new codes are expected to impact the compliance and enforcement mechanisms related to labour laws, potentially reducing regulatory burdens while enhancing transparency and accountability.

Currently, the labour law landscape in India is fragmented, with multiple overlapping and sometimes contradictory laws and regulations governing various aspects of employment. This complexity can pose significant challenges for employers and workers alike, hindering compliance and effective enforcement.

The Bharatiya Nyaya Sanhita, 2023, by consolidating and harmonizing various areas of law, including those related to labour and employment, could simplify the compliance landscape for employers. This could involve the establishment of a unified labour code, consolidating various existing laws and regulations into a cohesive and user-friendly framework.

Furthermore, the new codes may introduce streamlined reporting and record-keeping requirements, reducing the administrative burden on employers while promoting transparency and accountability. This could involve the adoption of digital platforms and online portals for submission of reports, maintenance of employee records, and filing of compliance-related documents.

The enforcement mechanisms under the new codes may also be strengthened, with provisions for enhanced monitoring, inspection, and deterrent penalties for non-compliance. This could include the establishment of specialized labour enforcement agencies or tribunals, equipped with the necessary resources and expertise to ensure effective implementation of labour laws.

Additionally, the new codes may promote greater collaboration and coordination among various regulatory bodies and stakeholders involved in labour law enforcement, fostering a more cohesive and effective approach to compliance monitoring and dispute resolution.

In conclusion, the Bharatiya Nyaya Sanhita, 2023, the Bharatiya Sakshya, 2023, and the Bharatiya Nagarik Suraksha Sanhita, 2023, represent a transformative shift in the legal landscape of India. Their impact on labour laws and their implementation is expected to be far-reaching and multifaceted, touching upon areas such as contract law, workplace safety, family rights, dispute resolution, emergency preparedness, critical infrastructure protection, evidentiary rules, worker protections, international alignment, and compliance mechanisms.

This comprehensive legal reform presents both challenges and opportunities for policymakers, employers, workers, and other stakeholders in the labour ecosystem. It necessitates a thorough review and harmonization of existing labour laws, fostering dialogue and collaboration among all parties involved. By embracing the principles of fairness, non-discrimination, and social justice enshrined in these codes, India has the potential to create a robust and progressive labour law framework that balances the interests of employers and workers, promotes decent work and sustainable economic growth, and positions the country as a responsible and compliant global partner.

As India continues to evolve and adapt to the changing global landscape, the impact of these new codes on labour laws will be significant. It is crucial for all stakeholders, including employers, employees, trade unions, policymakers, and legal professionals, to understand the implications of these reforms and navigate the changing legal terrain effectively.

This book aims to provide a comprehensive analysis of the impact of the Bharatiya Nyaya Sanhita, 2023, the Bharatiya Nagarik Suraksha Sanhita, 2023, and the Bharatiya Sakshya, 2023, on various aspects of labour laws in India. Through in-depth exploration of the provisions of these new codes, case studies, and practical implications, this book seeks to equip readers with the knowledge and understanding necessary to navigate the evolving labour law landscape in India.

By fostering a deeper understanding of the interconnections between these new codes and labour laws, this book aims to empower stakeholders to make informed decisions, ensure compliance, and advocate for necessary reforms to promote the rights, welfare, and dignity of workers while contributing to economic growth and social progress

Chapter 2

The Bharatiya Nyaya Sanhita, 2023

The Bharatiya Nyaya Sanhita, 2023, is a landmark legislation that represents a monumental effort to consolidate and codify the civil laws of India into a single, comprehensive, and cohesive framework. This ambitious endeavor, undertaken after years of deliberation and consultation with legal experts, academics, and stakeholders, aims to address the longstanding challenges posed by the fragmented and often overlapping nature of India's civil laws.

2.1 Objectives of the Bharatiya Nyaya Sanhita, 2023

The primary objectives of the Bharatiya Nyaya Sanhita, 2023, can be summarized as follows:

1. Consolidation and Harmonization: One of the central goals of the code is to consolidate and harmonize the various civil laws that have evolved over time, originating from diverse sources such as statutory laws, case laws, and customary practices. By bringing these disparate laws under a unified framework, the code seeks to eliminate inconsistencies, ambiguities, and overlapping jurisdictions that have plagued the legal system.

2. Clarity and Accessibility: The code endeavors to enhance clarity and accessibility for all stakeholders, including lawyers, judges, businesses, and the general public. By codifying civil laws in a comprehensive and organized manner, the code aims to reduce the complexity and uncertainty that often arise from interpreting multiple sources of law.

3. Uniformity and Consistency: Another critical objective is to promote uniformity and consistency in the application of civil

laws across different jurisdictions within India. This is particularly important in a diverse and federal nation like India, where variations in legal interpretations and practices can lead to disparities and inequalities.

4. Alignment with Contemporary Needs: The Bharatiya Nyaya Sanhita, 2023, acknowledges the evolving nature of society and aims to align civil laws with contemporary needs and realities. It incorporates modern legal principles, emerging trends, and societal developments to ensure the continued relevance and effectiveness of civil laws.

5. Fostering Economic Growth: By streamlining and modernizing civil laws, the code aims to create a more conducive legal environment for economic activities, facilitating ease of doing business, promoting investment, and supporting overall economic growth and development.

6. Promoting Social Justice: While pursuing economic objectives, the code also seeks to uphold the principles of social justice and equity. It incorporates provisions to protect the rights and interests of vulnerable and marginalized groups, ensuring that the legal framework promotes fairness and inclusivity.

2.2 Key Provisions of the Bharatiya Nyay Sanhita, 2023

The Bharatiya Nyaya Sanhita, 2023, stands as a towering achievement in India's legal landscape, a comprehensive and meticulously crafted code that seeks to consolidate and modernize the nation's civil laws. This monumental legislation, the culmination of years of deliberation and careful consideration, addresses a vast array of civil matters, reflecting the complexities of a rapidly evolving society and the ever-changing dynamics of human interactions.

1. Law of Contracts: At the heart of the Bharatiya Nyaya Sanhita, 2023, lies a robust framework for the law of contracts, a cornerstone of modern commerce and human endeavor. The code codifies the general principles of contract law, providing clarity and consistency in the formation, performance, breach, and remedies associated with contractual obligations.

The code's provisions on contract law are comprehensive, addressing the intricacies of offer and acceptance, consideration, capacity, legality, and the various modes of discharge, such as performance, agreement, or breach. It establishes guidelines for interpreting contractual terms, determining the intention of parties, and resolving ambiguities, thereby fostering certainty and predictability in contractual relationships.

Furthermore, the Bharatiya Nyaya Sanhita, 2023, recognizes the diverse nature of contracts and provides specific provisions for various types of contractual arrangements. These include, but are not limited to, sale of goods, lease agreements, service contracts, and construction contracts. The code offers tailored regulations to govern the unique aspects of each contract type, ensuring a robust and equitable legal framework for parties engaged in commercial transactions.

In a nod to the digital age, the code also addresses the burgeoning realm of e-contracts and digital transactions. It establishes guidelines for the formation, validity, and enforcement of electronic contracts, providing legal recognition and certainty to the virtual realm of commerce. Additionally, the code incorporates provisions for consumer protection and unfair trade practices, safeguarding the interests of consumers and promoting ethical business practices.

2. Law of Torts: The Bharatiya Nyaya Sanhita, 2023, also comprehensively addresses the law of torts, a crucial aspect of civil law that governs the redressal of wrongs and the allocation of liability for harmful conduct. The code codifies the general principles of tort law, including the foundational concepts of negligence, strict liability, and intentional torts.

Within its provisions, the code outlines the elements required to establish liability in tort cases, such as the existence of a duty of care, breach of that duty, causation, and the resulting harm or damage. It provides guidance on the assessment of damages, encompassing both compensatory and punitive measures, ensuring that victims of tortious conduct receive fair and adequate compensation.

The code delves into specific types of torts, offering tailored provisions for instances such as defamation, nuisance, and product liability. These sections address the nuances and unique considerations associated with each tort, providing clarity and guidance for adjudicating such cases.

Moreover, the Bharatiya Nyaya Sanhita, 2023, recognizes the evolving nature of tort law and incorporates provisions for emerging areas, such as environmental torts and cyber torts, ensuring that the legal framework remains relevant and responsive to the changing times.

3. Property Law: The realm of property law is a cornerstone of civil society, and the Bharatiya Nyaya Sanhita, 2023, dedicates substantial attention to this crucial area. The code offers comprehensive provisions for the ownership, transfer, and acquisition of immovable and movable property, establishing

clear guidelines and safeguards for these fundamental transactions.

The code's provisions on property law cover a wide range of topics, including the different types of ownership (sole, joint, co-ownership), the modes of acquiring property (purchase, gift, inheritance), and the various rights and obligations associated with property ownership. It addresses the intricacies of leases, mortgages, and other property-related transactions, ensuring that the legal framework remains robust and adaptable to the diverse needs of property owners and stakeholders.

Additionally, the Bharatiya Nyaya Sanhita, 2023, recognizes the significance of intellectual property rights in the modern era. It incorporates provisions for the protection of patents, trademarks, copyrights, and other forms of intellectual property, fostering innovation, creativity, and economic growth while safeguarding the rights of creators and innovators.

Furthermore, the code emphasizes the importance of environmental protection and sustainable development. It establishes regulations aimed at balancing property rights with environmental considerations, promoting responsible use of natural resources, and ensuring that development activities are carried out in an environmentally conscious manner.

4. Family Law: The Bharatiya Nyaya Sanhita, 2023, acknowledges the pivotal role of family in Indian society and dedicates substantial provisions to the realm of family law. The code codifies the laws related to marriage, divorce, adoption, and succession, providing a comprehensive and harmonized framework for these deeply personal and sensitive matters.

The code's provisions on marriage address the essential requirements, solemnization procedures, and the rights and obligations of spouses. It also offers guidance on the grounds for divorce, the legal process, and the distribution of assets and liabilities upon the dissolution of a marriage.

Adoption, a crucial aspect of family formation, is addressed in detail, with provisions outlining the eligibility criteria, procedures, and legal effects of adoption. The code also delves into the intricate matters of succession, inheritance, and the distribution of property among legal heirs, ensuring clarity and fairness in these often complex scenarios.

Moreover, the Bharatiya Nyaya Sanhita, 2023, recognizes the importance of protecting the rights and well-being of family members. It incorporates provisions for maintenance, guardianship, and child custody, prioritizing the best interests of children and vulnerable family members. Additionally, the code addresses the critical issue of domestic violence, establishing mechanisms for prevention, protection, and redressal.

In recognition of the sensitive nature of family matters, the code also provisions alternative dispute resolution mechanisms, such as mediation and conciliation, encouraging amicable resolutions and minimizing the emotional toll of protracted legal battles.

5. Commercial and Corporate Law: The Bharatiya Nyaya Sanhita, 2023, acknowledges the vital role of commerce and business in driving economic growth and prosperity. Consequently, it dedicates significant attention to the realm of commercial and corporate law, providing a robust legal framework for the formation, governance, and dissolution of companies and partnerships.

The code's provisions on corporate law address the intricate aspects of company formation, including the incorporation process, the drafting of memorandums and articles of association, and the allocation of share capital. It outlines the rights and responsibilities of shareholders, directors, and other stakeholders, fostering transparency and accountability in corporate governance.

Furthermore, the Bharatiya Nyaya Sanhita, 2023, offers guidance on corporate restructuring, mergers and acquisitions, and insolvency proceedings, ensuring that these complex transactions are conducted in a fair and orderly manner. It also incorporates provisions for competition law and anti-trust measures, promoting healthy market competition and safeguarding consumer interests.

In the realm of partnerships, the code provides a comprehensive framework for the formation, operation, and dissolution of various types of partnerships, including general partnerships, limited partnerships, and limited liability partnerships. It addresses the rights and obligations of partners, profit-sharing arrangements, and the mechanisms for dispute resolution within partnership structures.

2.3 Dispute Resolution:

Recognizing the importance of efficient and effective dispute resolution mechanisms, the Bharatiya Nyaya Sanhita, 2023, dedicates substantial provisions to civil procedure and the administration of justice. The code outlines the rules and procedures for filing civil cases, conducting trials, and pursuing appeals, ensuring fairness, transparency, and due process in the adjudication of disputes.

Moreover, the code acknowledges the growing importance of alternative dispute resolution (ADR) mechanisms, such as mediation and arbitration.

It incorporates provisions for the establishment and operation of ADR forums, encouraging parties to explore these cost-effective and time-efficient means of resolving disputes outside the traditional court system.

The Bharatiya Nyaya Sanhita, 2023, also addresses the crucial aspect of enforcement of judgments and decrees. It outlines the procedures and mechanisms for executing court orders, ensuring that the rule of law is upheld and that parties can obtain effective redressal for their grievances.

2.4 Liability and Compensation:

In the pursuit of justice and fairness, the Bharatiya Nyaya Sanhita, 2023, dedicates substantial attention to the intricate matter of liability and compensation in civil cases. The code establishes a comprehensive framework for determining liability, addressing the various factors that contribute to the attribution of responsibility, such as negligence, recklessness, or intentional wrongdoing.

The code's provisions on compensation aim to ensure that victims of civil wrongs receive adequate and appropriate redress for their losses and suffering. It outlines the principles and methods for calculating compensatory damages, taking into account factors such as economic losses, emotional distress, and the need for deterrence and punishment in egregious cases.

Furthermore, the Bharatiya Nyaya Sanhita, 2023, recognizes the unique circumstances where strict liability or no-fault compensation schemes may be warranted. It incorporates provisions for such scenarios, acknowledging that in certain contexts, the attribution of fault may be impractical or unjust, and compensation should be awarded based on the mere occurrence of harm or loss.

The code also addresses the growing importance of collective redressal mechanisms, such as class action suits. It establishes guidelines for the certification and conduct of class actions, ensuring that individuals with common grievances can collectively seek justice and compensation, promoting access to justice and deterring widespread harmful practices.

2.5 Regulatory Frameworks:

In recognition of the diverse and complex nature of modern society, the Bharatiya Nyaya Sanhita, 2023, incorporates provisions for the establishment and operation of regulatory bodies in various sectors. These regulatory frameworks aim to ensure the efficient and effective governance of industries, professions, and public interest domains, balancing the interests of stakeholders and promoting the greater good.

The code outlines the processes for creating and empowering regulatory bodies, defining their roles, responsibilities, and jurisdictions. It establishes guidelines for the appointment of regulators, the formulation of rules and regulations, and the enforcement of compliance measures within their respective domains.

Moreover, the Bharatiya Nyaya Sanhita, 2023, recognizes the importance of consumer protection, environmental protection, and other public interest concerns. It incorporates provisions for the establishment of regulatory bodies dedicated to these critical areas, ensuring that the rights and well-being of consumers are safeguarded, and that environmental sustainability is prioritized in the pursuit of economic development.

2.6 Transitional and Miscellaneous Provisions:

Acknowledging the monumental task of implementing such a comprehensive legal code, the Bharatiya Nyaya Sanhita, 2023, incorporates transitional and miscellaneous provisions to facilitate a smooth and orderly transition to the new legal regime.

The code offers guidelines for the interpretation and application of its provisions, providing clarity and consistency in the adjudication and enforcement of the new laws. It addresses potential conflicts or overlaps with existing laws, establishing a hierarchical framework for resolving such issues and ensuring legal certainty during the transition phase.

Furthermore, the Bharatiya Nyaya Sanhita, 2023, recognizes the dynamic nature of law and society, and incorporates provisions for periodic review and amendment of the code. It establishes mechanisms for gathering feedback, assessing the efficacy of the laws, and proposing revisions or updates as necessary, ensuring that the code remains relevant and responsive to the evolving needs of the nation.

2.7 Implications for Civil Disputes

The Bharatiya Nyaya Sanhita, 2023, with its comprehensive and unified approach to civil laws, has significant implications for the resolution of civil disputes, including those related to labour matters. Here are some potential implications:

1. Streamlining of Legal Procedures: The code aims to streamline legal procedures and reduce the complexity associated with civil disputes. By consolidating and harmonizing the applicable laws, the code simplifies the process of identifying and interpreting relevant legal provisions, potentially leading to more efficient and expeditious resolution of disputes.

2. Uniform Application of Laws: The code promotes uniformity and consistency in the application of civil laws across different jurisdictions within India. This uniformity can be particularly

beneficial in labour disputes, where employees and employers may operate across multiple states or regions, ensuring that legal interpretations and outcomes are consistent and predictable.

3. Clarity in Employment Contracts: The provisions of the code related to contract law can provide greater clarity and certainty in the interpretation and enforcement of employment contracts. This includes aspects such as non-compete clauses, severance agreements, and dispute resolution mechanisms, fostering better understanding and compliance among employers and employees.

4. Workplace Safety and Liability: The tort law provisions of the code may influence the application of labour laws related to workplace safety, liability for workplace accidents, and compensation mechanisms for occupational injuries or diseases. The code's provisions on strict liability and no-fault compensation schemes could potentially impact the way employers approach safety measures and employee protection.

5. Family-Related Provisions for Employees: The family law provisions in the code, such as those related to marriage, divorce, adoption, and succession, may have an impact on labour laws concerning maternity benefits, paternity leave, and other family-related provisions for employees. Employers and employees alike may need to understand and comply with these provisions to ensure compliance and protection of rights.

6. Dispute Resolution Mechanisms: The code establishes mechanisms for civil procedure and alternative dispute resolution, which can be applied to labour disputes as well. This includes provisions for mediation, arbitration, and other forms of

alternative dispute resolution, potentially providing more efficient and cost-effective means of resolving labour-related conflicts.

7. Enforcement of Judgments and Decrees: The provisions of the code related to the enforcement of judgments and decrees can have implications for the implementation of rulings and orders in labour disputes. Clear and consistent enforcement mechanisms can promote compliance and provide effective remedies for aggrieved parties.

8. Regulatory Frameworks and Public Interest: The code establishes regulatory frameworks and provisions for consumer protection, environmental protection, and other public interest domains. These provisions may influence labour laws and regulations aimed at protecting the rights and welfare of workers, ensuring safe working conditions, and promoting sustainable practices in various industries.

9. Interpretation and Application: The code provides guidelines for the interpretation and application of its provisions, which can impact how labour laws and regulations are interpreted and applied in practice. Consistency in interpretation and application can promote predictability and fairness in the resolution of labour disputes.

10. Transitional Provisions and Future Amendments: The transitional provisions of the code outline the process for its smooth implementation, while provisions for periodic review and amendment ensure its continued relevance. These provisions can impact the pace and extent of changes in labour laws, as well as

the ability to adapt to emerging trends and challenges in the realm of employment and labour relations.

It is important to note that the Bharatiya Nyaya Sanhita, 2023, is a comprehensive and far-reaching code, and its implications for labour laws may extend beyond the aspects mentioned above. As the code is implemented and interpreted, its full impact on labour-related matters will become more evident. Employers, employees, trade unions, and legal professionals will need to stay abreast of the developments and interpretations related to the code to effectively navigate the evolving legal landscape and ensure compliance with labour laws and regulations.

Chapter 3:

The Bharatiya Nagarik Suraksha Sanhita, 2023

In an increasingly complex and interconnected world, the need for comprehensive and robust civil protection measures has become paramount. The Bharatiya Nagarik Suraksha Sanhita, 2023, is a pioneering effort to establish a comprehensive framework for civil protection in India, addressing a wide range of issues related to public safety, disaster management, emergency response, and citizen welfare.

3.1 Objectives of the Bharatiya Nagarik Suraksha Sanhita, 2023

The primary objectives of the Bharatiya Nagarik Suraksha Sanhita, 2023, can be summarized as follows:

1. Enhancing Public Safety and Security: One of the core objectives of the code is to enhance public safety and security by establishing effective mechanisms for preventing, mitigating, and responding to potential threats and emergencies. This includes measures to address natural disasters, man-made calamities, acts of terrorism, civil unrest, and other security challenges.

2. Strengthening Disaster Preparedness and Response: The code aims to strengthen India's disaster preparedness and response capabilities by providing a comprehensive framework for disaster risk reduction, early warning systems, emergency management, and coordinated relief efforts. This is crucial in a country prone to various natural disasters, such as earthquakes, floods, and cyclones.

3. Protecting Critical Infrastructure: Recognizing the importance of critical infrastructure for the smooth functioning of modern societies, the code seeks to establish measures for the protection

of essential systems and assets, including power grids, communication networks, transportation systems, and other vital infrastructure.

4. Promoting Citizen Welfare and Resilience: The code emphasizes the importance of building resilient communities by promoting awareness, education, and capacity-building programs for citizens. By empowering individuals and communities with the knowledge and skills to prepare for and respond to emergencies, the code aims to enhance overall citizen welfare and resilience.

5. Ensuring Effective Coordination and Collaboration: The code recognizes the critical role of effective coordination and collaboration among various stakeholders, including government agencies, non-governmental organizations, private sector entities, and local communities. It establishes mechanisms for seamless communication, resource sharing, and joint decision-making processes to enhance the effectiveness of civil protection measures.

6. Aligning with International Best Practices: The Bharatiya Nagarik Suraksha Sanhita, 2023, seeks to align India's civil protection framework with international best practices and standards. By incorporating global guidelines and lessons learned from other countries, the code aims to ensure that India's civil protection measures are at par with global benchmarks and effectively address modern-day challenges.

3.2 Key Provisions of the Bharatiya Nagarik Suraksha Sanhita, 2023

Amidst the ever-present threats of natural and human-induced disasters, the Bharatiya Nagarik Suraksha Sanhita, 2023 (Indian Civil Protection

Code), stands as a beacon of resilience and preparedness for the nation. This comprehensive and forward-thinking legislation represents India's unwavering commitment to safeguarding the lives and well-being of its citizens, while also ensuring the protection of critical infrastructure and the continuity of essential services.

Disaster Risk Reduction: At the forefront of the Bharatiya Nagarik Suraksha Sanhita, 2023, lies a robust framework for disaster risk reduction, a proactive approach that acknowledges the importance of mitigating potential threats before they escalate into catastrophic events. The code establishes a national disaster risk reduction framework, encompassing methodologies for risk assessment, mitigation strategies, and capacity-building programs.

The provisions of the code mandate the integration of disaster risk reduction measures into land-use planning, building codes, and infrastructure development initiatives. By prioritizing hazard-resistant construction and sustainable urban planning, the code aims to create resilient communities that can withstand the impacts of disasters, minimizing loss of life and property.

Furthermore, the Bharatiya Nagarik Suraksha Sanhita, 2023, recognizes the inextricable link between disaster risk reduction and development policies. It incorporates regulations that mandate the integration of risk reduction strategies into all facets of development programs, ensuring that economic growth and progress do not come at the cost of increased vulnerability.

3.3 Early Warning Systems:

Timely and accurate information can save countless lives during emergencies and disasters. The Bharatiya Nagarik Suraksha Sanhita,

2023, emphasizes the critical importance of robust early warning systems, mandating their implementation for a wide range of potential hazards, including natural disasters, industrial accidents, and security threats.

The code's provisions encompass the collection, analysis, and dissemination of real-time data from various sources, such as weather monitoring stations, seismic networks, and intelligence agencies. This information is then rapidly communicated to relevant authorities and the public, enabling prompt action and evacuation measures when necessary.

Moreover, the Bharatiya Nagarik Suraksha Sanhita, 2023, recognizes the need for interoperability and coordination among early warning systems operated by different agencies and jurisdictions. It establishes regulations to ensure seamless information sharing and collaboration, breaking down silos and fostering a unified approach to early warning and emergency preparedness.

3.4 Emergency Management:

At the core of the Bharatiya Nagarik Suraksha Sanhita, 2023, lies a comprehensive emergency management framework, encompassing all phases of disaster response: prevention, preparedness, response, and recovery. The code mandates the development and implementation of emergency response plans at the national, state, and local levels, ensuring a coordinated and well-orchestrated approach to crisis management.

The provisions outline guidelines for the effective coordination of emergency services, including law enforcement, fire services, medical services, and search and rescue operations. This integrated approach aims to maximize resource utilization, streamline communication, and ensure a swift and efficient response to emergencies, minimizing loss of life and property.

Furthermore, the code addresses the critical aspects of emergency shelter management, evacuation procedures, and relief distribution. It establishes protocols for the identification and operation of safe shelters, the organized and orderly evacuation of affected areas, and the timely and equitable distribution of essential supplies and aid to those in need.

3.5 Critical Infrastructure Protection:

Recognizing the vital role of critical infrastructure in sustaining the nation's economic, social, and security interests, the Bharatiya Nagarik Suraksha Sanhita, 2023, dedicates significant attention to the protection of these essential assets and systems. The code mandates the identification and designation of critical infrastructure, encompassing sectors such as energy, transportation, telecommunications, and water supply.

The provisions outline comprehensive risk assessments, vulnerability analyses, and the implementation of robust security measures to safeguard these critical systems from various threats, including natural disasters, cyber-attacks, and acts of terrorism. The code also mandates the development and implementation of incident response plans and business continuity strategies, ensuring the rapid restoration of services and minimizing disruptions to essential operations.

Moreover, the Bharatiya Nagarik Suraksha Sanhita, 2023, recognizes the importance of public-private partnerships in critical infrastructure protection. It establishes guidelines for information sharing mechanisms and collaborative efforts between government agencies and private sector entities, fostering a coordinated and proactive approach to safeguarding the nation's vital assets.

3.6 Public Safety and Security:

In an era of evolving threats and complex security challenges, the Bharatiya Nagarik Suraksha Sanhita, 2023, establishes a robust national public safety and security framework. This comprehensive approach encompasses law enforcement, intelligence gathering, and counter-terrorism measures, ensuring a multi-layered defense against potential threats.

The code's provisions address crowd management, event security, and the protection of vulnerable locations and facilities, such as public spaces, transportation hubs, and critical infrastructure sites. It mandates the implementation of rigorous security protocols, surveillance measures, and specialized training for law enforcement personnel to effectively prevent and respond to security incidents.

Furthermore, the Bharatiya Nagarik Suraksha Sanhita, 2023, recognizes the ever-evolving nature of security threats, including cyber-attacks, and establishes regulations to enhance the nation's cyber security posture. It promotes the development of robust cyber defense mechanisms, information sharing protocols, and capacity-building initiatives to safeguard digital infrastructure and protect against cyber-enabled crimes.

3.7 Humanitarian Assistance and Relief:

In the aftermath of disasters and emergencies, the timely and effective provision of humanitarian assistance and relief is paramount. The Bharatiya Nagarik Suraksha Sanhita, 2023, addresses this critical aspect by establishing comprehensive provisions for the coordination and delivery of relief efforts.

The code outlines regulations for the management of relief supplies, temporary shelters, and the provision of essential services such as food, water, and medical aid. It mandates the establishment of robust supply chains, logistics networks, and distribution mechanisms to ensure that aid reaches those in need promptly and efficiently.

Moreover, the Bharatiya Nagarik Suraksha Sanhita, 2023, acknowledges the heightened vulnerability of certain segments of the population during emergencies. It incorporates guidelines for the protection of women, children, persons with disabilities, and other vulnerable groups, ensuring their safety, dignity, and access to essential services during relief operations.

3.8 Citizen Welfare and Resilience:

Recognizing that a truly resilient society is one where every citizen is empowered and prepared, the Bharatiya Nagarik Suraksha Sanhita, 2023, places significant emphasis on public awareness, education, and community engagement. The code mandates the establishment of comprehensive public awareness campaigns and educational programs to promote disaster preparedness and emergency response knowledge among citizens.

The provisions encourage the development of community-based disaster risk reduction initiatives, fostering a sense of ownership and responsibility among local communities. By involving citizens in the planning and implementation of civil protection measures, the code aims to create a culture of preparedness and resilience that permeates every level of society.

Furthermore, the Bharatiya Nagarik Suraksha Sanhita, 2023, recognizes the importance of capacity-building and training programs. It establishes regulations for the development of specialized training initiatives tailored to various stakeholders, including emergency responders, volunteers, and community leaders. These programs aim to enhance knowledge, skills, and capabilities, enabling a coordinated and effective response to emergencies and disasters.

3.9 Coordination and Collaboration:

The successful implementation of civil protection measures hinges on effective coordination and collaboration among various agencies and stakeholders. The Bharatiya Nagarik Suraksha Sanhita, 2023, acknowledges this critical imperative by establishing a national civil protection authority and mandating coordination mechanisms at various levels of government.

The code's provisions mandate the integration and collaboration of agencies such as civil defense, law enforcement, emergency services, and non-governmental organizations. It establishes frameworks for resource sharing, information exchange, and joint decision-making processes during emergencies, ensuring a unified and cohesive response.

Moreover, the Bharatiya Nagarik Suraksha Sanhita, 2023, recognizes the importance of vertical coordination, facilitating a seamless flow of information and directives between national, state, and local authorities. This integrated approach aims to optimize resource allocation, enhance situational awareness, and enable rapid and decisive action in the face of emergencies.

3.10 Legal and Regulatory Framework:

To provide a solid foundation for the implementation of civil protection measures, the Bharatiya Nagarik Suraksha Sanhita, 2023, establishes a comprehensive legal and regulatory framework. The code's provisions mandate the enactment of laws and regulations to support and enforce civil protection initiatives, ensuring compliance and accountability.

The code outlines penalties and sanctions for non-compliance with civil protection laws, serving as a deterrent and reinforcing the importance of adherence to established protocols and guidelines. Additionally, it incorporates provisions for the protection of civil rights and liberties during emergencies and disasters, striking a delicate balance between public safety and individual freedoms.

Furthermore, the Bharatiya Nagarik Suraksha Sanhita, 2023, acknowledges the need for periodic review and amendment of the legal and regulatory framework, ensuring that it remains relevant and responsive to evolving threats, technological advancements, and changing societal needs.

3.11 International Cooperation:

Disasters and emergencies often transcend national boundaries, necessitating a collaborative and coordinated global response. The Bharatiya Nagarik Suraksha Sanhita, 2023, recognizes this reality and establishes provisions for international cooperation and assistance in civil protection matters.

The code mandates the implementation of international agreements and conventions related to civil protection, facilitating cross-border coordination, information sharing, and the exchange of best practices and lessons learned. It establishes mechanisms for the facilitation of international relief efforts, enabling the smooth and efficient deployment of foreign aid and resources during emergencies.

Moreover, the Bharatiya Nagarik Suraksha Sanhita, 2023, encourages the participation of Indian agencies and experts in global forums and initiatives related to civil protection, promoting the exchange of knowledge and expertise on a global scale. This collaborative approach ensures that India remains at the forefront of civil protection efforts, contributing to and benefiting from the collective wisdom of the international community.

In a world where the threats of natural and human-induced disasters loom large, the Bharatiya Nagarik Suraksha Sanhita, 2023, stands as a beacon of hope and resilience. This comprehensive and forward-thinking legislation represents India's unwavering commitment to safeguarding its citizens, protecting critical infrastructure, and ensuring the continuity of essential services in the face of adversity.

Through its holistic approach, encompassing disaster risk reduction, early warning systems, emergency management, critical infrastructure protection, public safety and security, humanitarian assistance, citizen welfare, coordination, legal frameworks, and international cooperation, the Bharatiya Nagarik Suraksha Sanhita, 2023, lays the foundation for a safer and more resilient nation.

Its provisions mandate the integration of civil protection measures into all facets of governance, development, and societal life, fostering a culture of preparedness and resilience that permeates every level of society. By empowering citizens, strengthening institutional capacities, and promoting collaborative efforts, this landmark legislation aims to create a future where emergencies and disasters are met with unwavering resolve, swift action, and an unwavering commitment to protecting the lives, livelihoods, and well-being of all Indians.

In the face of an ever-changing landscape of risks and challenges, the Bharatiya Nagarik Suraksha Sanhita, 2023, stands as a testament to

India's determination to build a safer, more resilient, and more secure nation, one that is prepared to withstand the tests of time and emerge stronger in the face of adversity.

3.12 Implications for Civil Protection Measures

The Bharatiya Nagarik Suraksha Sanhita, 2023, has far-reaching implications for civil protection measures across various sectors, including labour and employment. Here are some potential implications:

1. Workplace Safety and Emergency Preparedness: The provisions of the code related to disaster risk reduction, early warning systems, and emergency management can have a direct impact on workplace safety and emergency preparedness measures in various industries and sectors. Employers may be required to adopt and implement emergency response plans, evacuation procedures, and other safety measures in accordance with the guidelines set forth by the code.

2. Critical Infrastructure Protection and Essential Services: The code's provisions on critical infrastructure protection may influence labour laws and regulations governing essential services and industries deemed critical for public safety and national security. This could include sectors such as energy, transportation, telecommunications, and healthcare, among others. Employers in these sectors may need to comply with specific security measures and incident response protocols outlined in the code.

3. Worker Safety and Protection: The code's emphasis on public safety and security measures, including those related to crowd management, event security, and the protection of vulnerable locations and facilities, could have implications for worker safety

and protection in various industries. Employers may need to ensure compliance with security protocols and safety measures to safeguard their employees in accordance with the code's provisions.

4. Relief and Assistance for Workers: The provisions of the code related to humanitarian assistance and relief efforts could potentially extend to the provision of aid and support for workers affected by emergencies or disasters. This could include temporary shelters, essential services, and other forms of assistance to ensure the well-being and protection of employees during and after such events.

5. Capacity Building and Training: The code's focus on citizen welfare and resilience, including public awareness and education programs, could lead to the development of training and capacity-building initiatives specifically tailored for workers in various industries. Employers may be required or encouraged to provide training and education to their employees on disaster preparedness, emergency response, and personal resilience.

6. Coordination and Collaboration: The code's provisions for coordination and collaboration among various stakeholders could facilitate better communication and information sharing between employers, labour unions, and relevant government agencies during emergencies or disasters. This could help in the effective implementation of civil protection measures and ensure the safety and well-being of workers.

7. Legal and Regulatory Compliance: The establishment of legal and regulatory frameworks under the code may require employers to

comply with specific civil protection laws, regulations, and guidelines related to their respective industries or sectors. This could include compliance with safety standards, emergency response protocols, and reporting requirements, among others.

8. International Cooperation and Cross-Border Implications: For industries and sectors with international operations or supply chains, the code's provisions for international cooperation and assistance in civil protection matters could have implications for cross-border coordination and the management of emergencies or disasters involving international workers or operations.

It is important to note that the implications of the Bharatiya Nagarik Suraksha Sanhita, 2023, on labour and employment-related matters may vary across different industries and sectors, depending on the specific nature of the work, the potential risks involved, and the criticality of the services provided. As the code is implemented and interpreted, further guidance and regulations specific to various industries and sectors may be developed to ensure effective integration of civil protection measures into labour laws and workplace practices.

Employers, employees, trade unions, and policymakers will need to stay abreast of the developments and interpretations related to the code, and work collaboratively to address the implications for labour and employment. By fostering a culture of preparedness, safety, and resilience in the workplace, the objectives of the Bharatiya Nagarik Suraksha Sanhita, 2023, can be effectively realized, ensuring the protection and well-being of workers while promoting overall public safety and security.

Chapter 4:

The Bharatiya Sakshya, 2023

The Bharatiya Sakshya, 2023, is a groundbreaking reform in the realm of evidentiary laws in India. This comprehensive code consolidates and modernizes the rules governing the admissibility, relevance, and weight of evidence in legal proceedings, ensuring fairness, transparency, and alignment with international best practices.

Prior to the enactment of this code, India's evidentiary laws were primarily governed by the Indian Evidence Act of 1872, which, despite numerous amendments over the years, had become outdated and inadequate to address the complexities of modern legal proceedings. The Bharatiya Sakshya, 2023, seeks to address these limitations by introducing a comprehensive and forward-looking framework for evidentiary rules, drawing upon contemporary legal principles, technological advancements, and evolving societal norms.

4.1 Objectives of the Bharatiya Sakshya, 2023

The primary objectives of the Bharatiya Sakshya, 2023, can be summarized as follows:

1. Streamlining the Evidentiary Process: One of the key objectives of the code is to streamline the evidentiary process and reduce the time and resources spent on procedural matters. By clearly defining the rules for admissibility of evidence and establishing guidelines for the evaluation of different types of evidence, the code aims to enhance efficiency and expedite legal proceedings.

2. Addressing Technological Advancements: The code recognizes the profound impact of technological advancements on the nature and types of evidence presented in legal proceedings. It seeks to

establish clear guidelines for the admissibility and authentication of electronic evidence, ensuring that legal proceedings can effectively handle modern forms of evidence while maintaining the integrity of the evidentiary process.

3. Promoting Fairness and Due Process: The Bharatiya Sakshya, 2023, places a strong emphasis on promoting fairness and due process in legal proceedings. It incorporates provisions related to the exclusion of illegally obtained evidence, the protection of privileged communication, and the rights of witnesses and victims, among other safeguards, to uphold the principles of justice and human rights.

4. Enhancing Credibility and Reliability: The code aims to enhance the credibility and reliability of evidence by establishing standards and procedures for the evaluation and weighing of different types of evidence. This includes provisions for expert testimony, scientific evidence, and the assessment of witness credibility, ensuring that legal decisions are based on sound and trustworthy evidence.

5. Aligning with International Standards: The Bharatiya Sakshya, 2023, seeks to align India's evidentiary laws with international standards and best practices. By incorporating principles and guidelines from well-established legal systems and international conventions, the code aims to facilitate cross-border cooperation and promote harmonization in the realm of evidentiary rules.

6. Fostering Judicial Efficiency and Consistency: The code aims to foster judicial efficiency and consistency by providing a clear and comprehensive framework for evidentiary rules. By reducing

ambiguities and inconsistencies in the application of evidentiary laws, the code seeks to promote predictability and uniformity in legal proceedings across different jurisdictions within India.

4.2 Key Provisions of the Bharatiya Sakshya, 2023

The Bharatiya Sakshya, 2023, is a comprehensive code that addresses various aspects of evidentiary laws. Here are some of the key provisions and areas covered by the code:

1. Admissibility of Evidence:
   - Comprehensive provisions defining the criteria for the admissibility of different types of evidence, including documentary evidence, physical evidence, testimonial evidence, and electronic evidence.
   - Guidelines for the authentication and verification of evidence to ensure its reliability and credibility.
   - Regulations for the exclusion of illegally obtained evidence and the protection of privileged communication.

2. Electronic Evidence:
   - Clear guidelines for the admissibility and authentication of electronic evidence, such as digital documents, emails, social media data, and other forms of electronic communication.
   - Provisions for the preservation and handling of electronic evidence to maintain its integrity and prevent tampering.
   - Regulations for the use of digital forensic techniques and expert testimony in the analysis of electronic evidence.

3. Expert Testimony and Scientific Evidence:

- o Provisions for the admissibility and evaluation of expert testimony in various fields, including forensics, medicine, engineering, and other scientific disciplines.
- o Guidelines for the qualification and credentialing of expert witnesses.
- o Regulations for the presentation and evaluation of scientific evidence, including statistical analyses, simulations, and other forms of scientific data.

4. Witness Testimony and Credibility:
   - o Comprehensive provisions governing the examination and cross-examination of witnesses.
   - o Guidelines for assessing witness credibility, including factors such as bias, memory, and consistency.
   - o Regulations for the protection of vulnerable witnesses, such as children, victims of abuse, and individuals with disabilities.

5. Privileged Communication:
   - o Provisions defining the scope and limitations of privileged communication, including attorney-client privilege, spousal privilege, and other recognized forms of confidential communication.
   - o Guidelines for the protection of privileged information and the circumstances under which it may be disclosed or waived.

6. Burden of Proof and Standard of Evidence:

- o Clear definitions and guidelines for the burden of proof and standard of evidence required in different types of legal proceedings, including civil and criminal cases.
- o Provisions for the allocation of the burden of proof and the shifting of the burden based on specific circumstances or presumptions.

7. Demonstrative Evidence and Exhibits:
   - o Regulations for the presentation and admissibility of demonstrative evidence, such as models, simulations, and visual aids.
   - o Guidelines for the proper handling, labeling, and preservation of physical exhibits.

8. Hearsay Evidence and Exceptions:
   - o Comprehensive provisions defining hearsay evidence and the general rule against its admissibility.
   - o Detailed exceptions to the hearsay rule, including specific situations where hearsay evidence may be admissible, such as dying declarations, spontaneous utterances, and business records.

9. Relevance and Probative Value:
   - o Guidelines for determining the relevance of evidence and its probative value in relation to the issues at hand.
   - o Provisions for the exclusion of evidence that is irrelevant, prejudicial, or otherwise lacking in probative value.

10. Judicial Discretion and Interpretation:
    - o Provisions granting judicial discretion in the interpretation and application of evidentiary rules, allowing judges to

consider the specific circumstances and interests of justice.

○ Guidelines for the balancing of competing interests and the exercise of judicial discretion in evidentiary matters.

4.3 Evidentiary laws of the Bharatiya Sakshya, 2023,

4.3.1 General Provisions

Article 1: Purpose and Scope

1.1 The Bharatiya Sakshya, 2023, establishes a comprehensive framework for the admissibility, relevance, and evaluation of evidence in all legal proceedings within the territory of India.

1.2 The code shall apply to all civil, criminal, administrative, and other judicial or quasi-judicial proceedings, unless otherwise specified by law.

1.3 The provisions of this code shall be interpreted and applied in a manner that promotes fairness, transparency, and the effective administration of justice.

Article 2: Definitions

2.1 "Evidence" shall mean any relevant information, whether oral, written, or physical, that is presented before a court or tribunal for the purpose of proving or disproving a fact or issue in dispute.

2.2 "Admissible evidence" shall mean evidence that is deemed permissible and acceptable by the court or tribunal in accordance with the provisions of this code and other applicable laws.

2.3 "Relevant evidence" shall mean evidence that has a tendency to make the existence of a fact or issue more probable or less probable than it would be without the evidence.

2.4 "Probative value" shall mean the degree to which evidence tends to prove or disprove a fact or issue in dispute.

2.5 "Privileged communication" shall mean confidential communication protected by law from disclosure in legal proceedings.

Article 3: Fundamental Principles

3.1 All relevant evidence shall be admissible, unless otherwise provided by this code or other applicable laws.

3.2 Evidence shall be evaluated based on its relevance, probative value, and reliability, taking into account the specific circumstances of each case.

3.3 The court or tribunal shall have the discretion to exclude evidence if its probative value is substantially outweighed by the risk of unfair prejudice, confusion of issues, or undue delay in the proceedings.

3.4 The burden of proof shall be allocated in accordance with the applicable substantive law and procedural rules governing the specific legal proceeding.

4.3.2 Admissibility of Evidence

Article 4: General Rules of Admissibility

4.1 Evidence shall be admissible if it is relevant to the facts or issues in dispute and is not otherwise excluded by this code or other applicable laws.

4.2 Evidence shall be deemed relevant if it has a tendency to make the existence of a fact or issue more probable or less probable than it would be without the evidence.

4.3 The court or tribunal shall have the discretion to exclude relevant evidence if its probative value is substantially outweighed by the risk of unfair prejudice, confusion of issues, or undue delay in the proceedings.

Article 5: Illegally Obtained Evidence

5.1 Evidence obtained in violation of fundamental rights or through illegal means shall be inadmissible, unless the court or tribunal determines that the admission of such evidence is necessary to protect a significant public interest or to ensure the fairness of the proceedings.

5.2 In determining the admissibility of illegally obtained evidence, the court or tribunal shall consider the nature and severity of the violation, the significance of the evidence, and the interests of justice.

Article 6: Privileged Communication

6.1 Confidential communication between certain persons or entities shall be protected by privilege and shall not be subject to disclosure in legal proceedings, unless the privilege is waived or an exception applies.

6.2 The following types of communication shall be considered privileged, subject to specific limitations and exceptions:

a) Attorney-client privilege

b) Spousal privilege

c) Physician-patient privilege

d) Clergy-penitent privilege

e) Journalist-source privilege

f) Government privilege

g) Other privileges recognized by law or established by the court or tribunal.

6.3 The court or tribunal shall have the discretion to determine the scope and application of privileges, taking into account the specific circumstances of each case and the interests of justice.

Article 7: Hearsay Evidence

7.1 Hearsay evidence, defined as a statement made outside of the current legal proceeding and offered to prove the truth of the matter asserted, shall generally be inadmissible, subject to specific exceptions provided in this code.

7.2 The following shall be considered exceptions to the hearsay rule, and such evidence may be admissible:

a) Spontaneous utterances or excited utterances made under the stress or excitement of an event or condition

b) Dying declarations made by a person under the belief of impending death

c) Business records or other records kept in the regular course of business or official activities

d) Statements against interest made by a person that are contrary to their own interests

e) Prior statements made by a witness or party that are inconsistent with their current testimony

f) Statements made for the purpose of medical diagnosis or treatment

g) Other exceptions recognized by law or established by the court or tribunal.

7.3 The court or tribunal shall have the discretion to determine the admissibility of hearsay evidence based on its relevance, probative value, and the specific circumstances of each case.

4.3.3 Types of Evidence

Article 8: Documentary Evidence

8.1 Documentary evidence, including written or printed materials, records, and other data compilations, shall be admissible if authenticated and relevant to the facts or issues in dispute.

8.2 The authentication of documentary evidence may be established through various means, including:

a) Testimony of a witness with knowledge of the document's origin or contents

b) Comparison with authenticated specimens or other evidence

c) Distinctive characteristics or circumstances indicating authenticity

d) Compliance with statutory or regulatory requirements for authentication

e) Other methods recognized by law or established by the court or tribunal.

8.3 The court or tribunal shall have the discretion to determine the admissibility and weight of documentary evidence based on its relevance, authenticity, and the specific circumstances of each case.

Article 9: Physical Evidence

9.1 Physical evidence, including tangible objects, substances, or materials, shall be admissible if relevant to the facts or issues in dispute and properly authenticated.

9.2 The authentication of physical evidence may be established through various means, including:

a) Testimony of a witness with knowledge of the origin, custody, or condition of the evidence

b) Identification through distinctive characteristics or markings

c) Scientific or forensic analysis or testing

d) Compliance with statutory or regulatory requirements for authentication

e) Other methods recognized by law or established by the court or tribunal.

9.3 The court or tribunal shall have the discretion to determine the admissibility and weight of physical evidence based on its relevance, authenticity, and the specific circumstances of each case.

Article 10: Testimonial Evidence

10.1 Testimonial evidence, including oral statements or depositions given by witnesses under oath or affirmation, shall be admissible if relevant to the facts or issues in dispute.

10.2 The court or tribunal shall have the discretion to assess the credibility and weight of testimonial evidence based on various factors, including:

a) The witness's opportunity to observe or perceive the relevant events or facts

b) The witness's ability to remember and accurately relate the observed events or facts

c) The witness's demeanor, bias, or interest in the outcome of the case

d) The consistency or inconsistency of the witness's testimony with other evidence

e) The presence or absence of corroborating or contradictory evidence

f) Other factors relevant to the reliability and credibility of the witness's testimony.

10.3 The court or tribunal shall have the authority to control the examination and cross-examination of witnesses, including the scope, order, and manner of questioning.

Article 11: Electronic Evidence

11.1 Electronic evidence, including data, records, or information stored or transmitted in digital form, shall be admissible if relevant to the facts or issues in dispute and properly authenticated.

11.2 The authentication of electronic evidence may be established through various means, including:

a) Testimony of a witness with knowledge of the creation, storage, or transmission of the electronic evidence

b) Identification through distinctive characteristics or metadata

c) Compliance with statutory or regulatory requirements for authentication

d) Application of reliable forensic techniques or tools for digital evidence analysis

e) Other methods recognized by law or established by the court or tribunal.

11.3 The court or tribunal shall have the discretion to determine the admissibility and weight of electronic evidence based on its relevance, authenticity, and the specific circumstances of each case, taking into account the reliability and integrity of the electronic evidence.

Article 12: Expert Testimony and Scientific Evidence

12.1 Expert testimony and scientific evidence shall be admissible if relevant to the facts or issues in dispute, and the expert witness or scientific methodology employed is deemed reliable and appropriate by the court or tribunal.

12.2 The court or tribunal shall have the discretion to assess the qualifications, expertise, and credibility of expert witnesses, as well as the reliability and relevance of their testimony or scientific evidence.

12.3 In determining the admissibility and weight of expert testimony or scientific evidence, the court or tribunal may consider factors such as:

a) The expert's qualifications, experience, and specialized knowledge in the relevant field

b) The reliability and validity of the methods, techniques, or principles employed by the expert

c) The extent to which the expert's methodology or findings have been subject to peer review or scrutiny within the relevant scientific community

d) The potential for bias, conflict of interest, or other factors that may affect the expert's objectivity

e) The relevance and probative value of the expert's testimony or scientific evidence to the facts or issues in dispute

f) Other factors relevant to the reliability and credibility of the expert's testimony or scientific evidence.

12.4 The court or tribunal shall have the authority to limit or exclude expert testimony or scientific evidence if it is deemed unreliable, irrelevant, or if its probative value is substantially outweighed by the risk of unfair prejudice, confusion of issues, or undue delay in the proceedings.

4.3.4 Evaluation and Weighing of Evidence

Article 13: Relevance and Probative Value

13.1 The court or tribunal shall evaluate the relevance and probative value of all admissible evidence in determining the facts and issues in dispute.

13.2 Relevant evidence shall be admissible unless its probative value is substantially outweighed by the risk of unfair prejudice, confusion of issues, or undue delay in the proceedings.

13.3 In assessing the probative value of evidence, the court or tribunal shall consider factors such as:

a) The degree to which the evidence tends to prove or disprove a material fact or issue in dispute

b) The reliability and credibility of the evidence and its source

c) The existence of corroborating or contradictory evidence

d) The potential for the evidence to be misused, misinterpreted, or to cause unfair prejudice

e) Other factors relevant to the weight and persuasiveness of the evidence.

Article 14: Weighing of Evidence

14.1 The court or tribunal shall weigh and evaluate all admissible evidence in its entirety, considering its relevance, probative value, and credibility, and shall determine the facts and issues in dispute based on a preponderance of the evidence.

14.2 In weighing the evidence, the court or tribunal shall consider factors such as:

a) The consistency or inconsistency of the evidence with other evidence

b) The presence or absence of corroborating or contradictory evidence

c) The credibility and reliability of witnesses or sources of evidence

d) The plausibility or implausibility of the evidence in light of other facts or circumstances

e) The potential for bias, interest, or other factors that may affect the reliability of the evidence

f) Other factors relevant to the weight and persuasiveness of the evidence.

14.3 The court or tribunal shall have the discretion to determine the appropriate weight and persuasiveness to be accorded to each piece of evidence, taking into account the specific circumstances of the case and the interests of justice.

Article 15: Burden of Proof and Standard of Evidence

15.1 The burden of proof shall be allocated in accordance with the applicable substantive law and procedural rules governing the specific legal proceeding.

15.2 In civil cases, the burden of proof shall generally be on the party asserting a claim or allegation, and the standard of proof shall be a preponderance of the evidence, unless otherwise specified by law.

15.3 In criminal cases, the burden of proof shall be on the prosecution to establish the guilt of the accused beyond a reasonable doubt, unless otherwise specified by law.

15.4 The court or tribunal shall have the discretion to determine the allocation and shifting of the burden of proof based on specific presumptions, inferences, or other circumstances recognized by law or established in the specific case.

4.3.5 Demonstrative and Illustrative Evidence

Article 16: Admissibility of Demonstrative and Illustrative Evidence

16.1 Demonstrative and illustrative evidence, such as models, simulations, diagrams, or other visual aids, may be admissible to assist the court or tribunal in understanding or evaluating other admissible evidence.

16.2 The court or tribunal shall have the discretion to determine the admissibility and appropriate use of demonstrative or illustrative evidence based on its relevance, accuracy, and potential to assist in the understanding or evaluation of other admissible evidence.

16.3 In determining the admissibility and weight of demonstrative or illustrative evidence, the court or tribunal may consider factors such as:

a) The accuracy and reliability of the demonstrative or illustrative evidence in representing or depicting the relevant facts or issues

b) The potential for the demonstrative or illustrative evidence to be misleading, confusing, or unfairly prejudicial

c) The qualifications or expertise of the person(s) responsible for creating or presenting the demonstrative or illustrative evidence

d) The extent to which the demonstrative or illustrative evidence is based on or supported by other admissible evidence

e) Other factors relevant to the probative value and reliability of the demonstrative or illustrative evidence.

Article 17: Handling and Preservation of Exhibits

17.1 All physical exhibits or items of evidence admitted in legal proceedings shall be properly labeled, cataloged, and preserved to maintain their integrity and prevent tampering or alteration.

17.2 The court or tribunal shall establish procedures and protocols for the proper handling, storage, and preservation of physical exhibits or items of evidence, taking into account the nature and characteristics of the evidence.

17.3 The parties to the legal proceeding shall have the right to inspect and examine physical exhibits or items of evidence, subject to appropriate safeguards and restrictions as determined by the court or tribunal.

17.4 The court or tribunal shall have the authority to impose sanctions or take appropriate measures in cases of tampering, destruction, or improper handling of physical exhibits or items of evidence.

4.3.6 Judicial Discretion and Interpretation

Article 18: Exercise of Judicial Discretion

18.1 The court or tribunal shall have the discretion to interpret and apply the provisions of this code in a manner that promotes fairness, transparency, and the effective administration of justice.

18.2 In exercising its discretion, the court or tribunal shall consider the specific circumstances of each case, the interests of justice, and the principles and objectives underlying this code.

18.3 The court or tribunal shall have the authority to make evidentiary rulings, including the admission, exclusion, or limitation of evidence, as well as the determination of the weight and persuasiveness to be accorded to the evidence.

18.4 The exercise of judicial discretion shall be subject to appellate review in accordance with established legal procedures and standards.

Article 19: Interpretation and Application

19.1 The provisions of this code shall be interpreted and applied in a manner that is consistent with the Constitution of India, international treaties and conventions ratified by India, and other applicable laws and principles of law.

19.2 In interpreting and applying the provisions of this code, the court or tribunal may consider relevant judicial precedents, legal scholarship, and international best practices in the field of evidentiary laws.

19.3 In cases where the provisions of this code are ambiguous or silent on a particular evidentiary issue, the court or tribunal shall have the discretion to interpret and apply the code in a manner that promotes justice, fairness, and the effective administration of legal proceedings.

4.3.7 Transitional and Final Provisions

Article 20: Repeal and Savings

20.1 The Indian Evidence Act of 1872, and all other laws or provisions relating to the admissibility and evaluation of evidence, shall stand repealed upon the commencement of this code.

20.2 Notwithstanding the repeal of the Indian Evidence Act of 1872 and other related laws, all legal proceedings initiated prior to the commencement of this code shall continue to be governed by the applicable laws and evidentiary rules in force at the time of initiation of such proceedings.

20.3 Any action taken, order issued, or decision made in relation to evidentiary matters under the repealed laws shall continue to be valid and effective, unless specifically reviewed or modified in accordance with the provisions of this code.

Article 21: Commencement and Implementation

21.1 This code shall come into force on a date to be notified by the Central Government.

21.2 The Central Government may, by notification, make rules for carrying out the provisions of this code and for providing for any matter relating to the admissibility, relevance, and evaluation of evidence.

21.3 The High Courts may, in consultation with the Central Government, issue practice directions or guidelines for the effective implementation and application of this code within their respective jurisdictions.

Article 22: Review and Amendment

22.1 The Central Government shall establish a committee or commission to periodically review

22.2 The committee or commission shall assess the implementation and effectiveness of this code, identify areas for improvement, and recommend amendments or revisions as necessary to ensure that the code remains relevant, efficient, and aligned with evolving legal principles and societal needs.

22.3 The Central Government shall consider the recommendations of the committee or commission and may, through due legislative process, amend or revise the provisions of this code as deemed appropriate.

4.3.8 Supplementary Provisions

Article 23: Application to Specific Types of Proceedings

23.1 In addition to the general provisions of this code, specific rules or guidelines may be established for the admissibility, relevance, and evaluation of evidence in specialized legal proceedings, such as:

  a) Criminal proceedings

  b) Civil proceedings

  c) Family law proceedings

  d) Administrative or regulatory proceedings

  e) Arbitration or alternative dispute resolution proceedings

  f) Proceedings involving juveniles or vulnerable individuals

  g) Proceedings related to specific subject matters or areas of law

23.2 The Central Government, in consultation with relevant stakeholders and experts, shall have the authority to promulgate rules or guidelines for the application of this code to specific types of legal proceedings, taking into account the unique nature, requirements, and considerations of such proceedings.

Article 24: Protection of Witnesses and Victims

24.1 The court or tribunal shall have the authority to implement measures for the protection of witnesses, victims, and other vulnerable individuals involved in legal proceedings, including but not limited to:

a) Allowing for the use of closed-circuit television, video conferencing, or other remote testimony methods

b) Granting anonymity or non-disclosure of identifying information

c) Providing for in-camera or closed-door proceedings

d) Ordering the non-disclosure or redaction of sensitive or confidential information

e) Imposing limitations on the manner, scope, or extent of questioning or cross-examination

f) Other measures deemed necessary and appropriate to protect the safety, well-being, and privacy of witnesses, victims, or vulnerable individuals.

24.2 In determining the appropriate protective measures, the court or tribunal shall consider factors such as the risk of harm, intimidation, or retaliation, the vulnerability or special needs of the individual, and the interests of justice.

Article 25: International Cooperation and Assistance

25.1 The Central Government shall seek to facilitate international cooperation and assistance in matters related to the admissibility, relevance, and evaluation of evidence, including but not limited to:

a) Mutual legal assistance in the gathering, preservation, and exchange of evidence

b) Recognition and enforcement of foreign evidentiary orders or requests

c) Cooperation in the authentication and verification of evidence obtained from foreign jurisdictions

d) Participation in international conventions, treaties, or agreements related to evidentiary matters

e) Exchange of information, best practices, and expertise in the field of evidentiary laws and procedures.

25.2 The Central Government may enter into bilateral or multilateral agreements or arrangements with foreign countries or international organizations to further the objectives of international cooperation and assistance in evidentiary matters.

Article 26: Training and Capacity Building

26.1 The Central Government and relevant authorities shall undertake measures to promote training and capacity building initiatives for judges, lawyers, law enforcement officials, and other stakeholders in the legal system, with a focus on the effective implementation and application of this code.

26.2 Such training and capacity building initiatives may include, but are not limited to:

a) Seminars, workshops, and educational programs on the provisions and principles of this code

b) Development of teaching materials, manuals, and guidelines on evidentiary laws and procedures

c) Collaboration with academic institutions, legal associations, and subject matter experts

d) Continuing legal education programs for practicing lawyers and judicial officers

e) Exchange programs or study visits with foreign jurisdictions to learn about international best practices in evidentiary laws.

Article 27: Periodic Review and Reporting

27.1 The Central Government shall establish a mechanism for the periodic review and reporting on the implementation and effectiveness of this code, including the collection and analysis of data and statistics related to evidentiary matters.

27.2 The review and reporting process shall involve consultation with relevant stakeholders, such as the judiciary, legal professionals, law enforcement agencies, and civil society organizations, to gather feedback and identify areas for improvement.

27.3 The findings and recommendations from the periodic review and reporting shall be made publicly available and shall serve as a basis for further amendments, reforms, or capacity building initiatives related to evidentiary laws and procedures.

Article 28: Public Awareness and Legal Literacy

28.1 The Central Government and relevant authorities shall undertake measures to promote public awareness and legal literacy regarding the provisions and principles of this code, as well as the rights and obligations of individuals and entities in relation to evidentiary matters.

28.2 Such public awareness and legal literacy initiatives may include, but are not limited to:

a) Dissemination of information through various media channels, including print, broadcast, and digital platforms

b) Development of educational materials and resources in multiple languages and formats

c) Collaboration with civil society organizations, educational institutions, and community leaders

d) Incorporation of evidentiary laws and principles into relevant curricula and training programs

e) Establishment of helplines, legal aid clinics, or other support services to provide guidance on evidentiary matters.

Article 29: Regulations and Supplementary Guidelines

29.1 The Central Government may, by notification, make regulations or issue supplementary guidelines for the effective implementation and administration of this code.

29.2 Such regulations or supplementary guidelines may provide further clarification, elaboration, or procedural details on specific provisions of this code, taking into account the evolving needs, challenges, and developments in the field of evidentiary laws.

29.3 The regulations or supplementary guidelines shall be consistent with the principles, objectives, and provisions of this code and shall be subject to periodic review and revision as necessary.

This comprehensive recreation covers the key provisions and areas addressed by the Bharatiya Sakshya, 2023, including general principles, admissibility of evidence, types of evidence, evaluation and weighing of evidence, demonstrative and illustrative evidence, judicial discretion and interpretation, transitional and final provisions, as well as supplementary provisions related to specific proceedings, witness protection, international cooperation, training, periodic review, and public awareness.

4.4 Implications for Admissibility and Evaluation of Evidence

The Bharatiya Sakshya, 2023, has significant implications for the admissibility and evaluation of evidence in labour-related cases, which can impact the resolution of disputes, enforcement of labour laws, and the protection of workers' rights. Here are some potential implications:

1. Electronic Evidence in Labour Disputes: The provisions of the code related to electronic evidence can have a profound impact on labour-related cases. With the increasing use of digital communication and record-keeping in the workplace, electronic evidence such as emails, text messages, surveillance footage, and digital records may play a crucial role in establishing facts or supporting claims in labour disputes. The code's guidelines for the admissibility and authentication of electronic evidence can help ensure the fair and effective evaluation of such evidence in labour-related proceedings.

2. Expert Testimony and Scientific Evidence: The code's provisions for the admissibility and evaluation of expert testimony and scientific evidence can be particularly relevant in labour-related cases involving occupational health and safety, workplace injuries, or specialized technical matters. Expert witnesses from fields such as medicine, ergonomics, industrial hygiene, or engineering may provide crucial evidence in these cases, and the code's guidelines can help ensure the proper qualification and credibility of such experts, as well as the appropriate weighing of their testimony.

3. Witness Testimony and Credibility: Many labour-related cases heavily rely on witness testimony from employees, employers, or other individuals involved in the dispute. The code's provisions for the examination and cross-examination of witnesses, as well as the guidelines for assessing witness credibility, can play a significant role in ensuring the fair and impartial evaluation of such testimony in labour-related proceedings.

4. Privileged Communication: The provisions of the code related to privileged communication can have implications in labour-related cases involving confidential communication between employees and labour unions, legal counsel, or other protected parties. The code's guidelines can help ensure the protection of privileged information while also providing clarity on the circumstances under which such information may be disclosed or waived.

5. Burden of Proof and Standard of Evidence: The code's clear definitions and guidelines for the burden of proof and standard of evidence can be instrumental in labour-related cases, where the allocation of the burden of proof and the required level of evidence can significantly impact the outcome of the case. These provisions can help ensure consistency and fairness in the evaluation of evidence in labour disputes and other employment-related matters.

6. Demonstrative Evidence and Exhibits: In labour-related cases involving workplace accidents, safety violations, or other physical aspects of the work environment, demonstrative evidence and physical exhibits can play a critical role. The code's regulations for the presentation and admissibility of such evidence, as well as

the guidelines for proper handling and preservation of exhibits, can help ensure the fair and effective evaluation of this type of evidence in labour-related proceedings.

7. Hearsay Evidence and Exceptions: While hearsay evidence is generally inadmissible, the code's detailed exceptions to the hearsay rule may be relevant in certain labour-related cases. For example, spontaneous utterances made by an injured worker or business records related to employee records or safety protocols may be admissible under specific exceptions, and the code's provisions can provide guidance on the proper application of these exceptions.

8. Relevance and Probative Value: The code's guidelines for determining the relevance of evidence and its probative value can be crucial in labour-related cases, where the admission or exclusion of certain evidence can significantly impact the outcome of the case. The code's provisions can help ensure that only relevant and probative evidence is considered, while irrelevant or prejudicial evidence is excluded, promoting fairness and impartiality in the decision-making process.

9. Judicial Discretion and Interpretation: The code's provisions granting judicial discretion in the interpretation and application of evidentiary rules can be particularly important in labour-related cases, where the specific circumstances and competing interests may require a balanced and nuanced approach. The guidelines for the exercise of judicial discretion can help ensure that the interests of both employers and employees are adequately considered, while upholding the principles of justice and fairness.

It is important to note that the implications of the Bharatiya Sakshya, 2023, on labour-related cases may vary depending on the specific nature of the dispute, the type of evidence involved, and the jurisdiction in which the case is being heard. As the code is implemented and interpreted by courts and legal professionals, further clarifications and precedents may emerge, shaping the application of evidentiary rules in the context of labour and employment matters.

Employers, employees, trade unions, and legal professionals involved in labour-related cases will need to stay abreast of the developments and interpretations related to the code, and work collaboratively to ensure that the principles of fairness, transparency, and due process are upheld in the evaluation and admissibility of evidence. By fostering a deeper understanding of the evidentiary framework established by the Bharatiya Sakshya, 2023, stakeholders can contribute to the effective resolution of labour disputes and the protection of workers' rights while promoting the overall integrity of the legal system.

Chapter 5:

Impact on Labour Protection and Removal Rules

The enactment of the Bharatiya Nyaya Sanhita, 2023, the Bharatiya Nagarik Suraksha Sanhita, 2023, and the Bharatiya Sakshya, 2023, has far-reaching implications for labour protection and removal rules in India. These comprehensive codes aim to streamline and modernize various aspects of civil laws, civil protection measures, and evidentiary rules, respectively. However, their impact on labour laws and regulations is multifaceted, affecting crucial areas such as worker safety, compensation, grievance redressal mechanisms, and rules governing the removal or termination of employees.

Analysis of the Changes in Labour Protection Rules

The Bharatiya Nyaya Sanhita, 2023, seeks to consolidate and harmonize civil laws, including those related to torts, property rights, and liability. This has significant implications for labour protection rules, as it can influence the interpretation and enforcement of laws related to workplace safety, liability for occupational injuries or diseases, and compensation mechanisms.

One of the key changes introduced by the Bharatiya Nyaya Sanhita, 2023, is the codification of general principles of tort law, including negligence, strict liability, and intentional torts. This codification can have a direct impact on the application of labour laws related to workplace safety and employer liability. The code's provisions on strict liability and no-fault compensation schemes may potentially influence the way employers approach safety measures and employee protection.

Additionally, the code's provisions on property rights and the protection of intellectual property can have implications for labour protection rules in sectors where intellectual property plays a significant role. For instance, in industries relying heavily on trade secrets or proprietary information, the code's provisions may impact the way employers safeguard such information while balancing the rights and protections afforded to employees.

The Bharatiya Nagarik Suraksha Sanhita, 2023, focuses on civil protection measures, including disaster management, emergency response, and critical infrastructure protection. While the primary objective of this code is to enhance public safety and security, its provisions can also have implications for labour protection rules, particularly in sectors deemed critical for public safety and national security.

The code's emphasis on disaster risk reduction, early warning systems, and emergency management can lead to the development of robust workplace safety protocols and emergency response measures in various industries. Employers may be required to implement emergency response plans, evacuation procedures, and other safety measures in accordance with the guidelines set forth by the code.

Furthermore, the provisions of the Bharatiya Nagarik Suraksha Sanhita, 2023, related to critical infrastructure protection can influence labour laws and regulations governing essential services and industries deemed critical for public safety and national security. Employers in these sectors may need to comply with specific security measures, incident response protocols, and safety standards outlined in the code.

The Bharatiya Sakshya, 2023, focuses on modernizing evidentiary rules and has implications for the admissibility and evaluation of evidence in legal proceedings, including those related to labour disputes. The code's provisions on electronic evidence, expert testimony, and witness credibility can impact the way evidence is presented and evaluated in cases involving workplace accidents, safety violations, or other labour-related matters.

The code's guidelines for the admissibility and authentication of electronic evidence can help ensure the fair and effective evaluation of digital records, surveillance footage, and other forms of electronic evidence in labour-related cases. Similarly, the code's provisions on expert testimony and scientific evidence can be particularly relevant in cases involving occupational health and safety, workplace injuries, or specialized technical matters.

Overall, the analysis of the changes introduced by these three codes reveals a multifaceted impact on labour protection rules. While the primary objectives of these codes may not be directly focused on labour laws, their provisions have significant implications for worker safety, compensation mechanisms, and the overall legal framework governing labour protection in India.

Implications for Worker Safety, Compensation, and Grievance Redressal Mechanisms

The changes brought about by the Bharatiya Nyaya Sanhita, 2023, the Bharatiya Nagarik Suraksha Sanhita, 2023, and the Bharatiya Sakshya, 2023, have far-reaching implications for worker safety, compensation, and grievance redressal mechanisms. These implications can be explored through the following perspectives:

Worker Safety:

1. Strict Liability and No-Fault Compensation Schemes: The Bharatiya Nyaya Sanhita, 2023's provisions on strict liability and

no-fault compensation schemes can potentially influence the way employers approach worker safety measures. Employers may be incentivized to implement more rigorous safety protocols and preventive measures to mitigate potential liabilities arising from workplace accidents or occupational injuries.

2. Workplace Emergency Preparedness: The Bharatiya Nagarik Suraksha Sanhita, 2023's emphasis on disaster risk reduction, early warning systems, and emergency management can lead to enhanced workplace emergency preparedness measures. Employers may be required to develop and implement emergency response plans, evacuation procedures, and other safety measures to ensure the safety of workers in the event of natural disasters, fires, or other emergencies.

3. Critical Infrastructure Protection: For industries and sectors deemed critical for public safety and national security, the provisions of the Bharatiya Nagarik Suraksha Sanhita, 2023, related to critical infrastructure protection can result in heightened security measures and incident response protocols. These measures can contribute to improved worker safety by mitigating potential risks and ensuring a more secure work environment.

Compensation:

1. Liability and Compensation Mechanisms: The Bharatiya Nyaya Sanhita, 2023's provisions on liability and compensation can impact the mechanisms for compensating workers in the event of workplace accidents, occupational injuries, or diseases. The code's provisions on no-fault compensation schemes may facilitate more streamlined and efficient compensation processes,

ensuring that workers receive timely and appropriate compensation.

2. Evidence in Compensation Claims: The Bharatiya Sakshya, 2023's provisions on the admissibility and evaluation of evidence can have implications for compensation claims related to workplace incidents. The code's guidelines on electronic evidence, expert testimony, and witness credibility can help ensure that compensation claims are evaluated fairly and based on credible evidence.

3. Uniformity and Consistency: The consolidation and harmonization of civil laws under the Bharatiya Nyaya Sanhita, 2023, can promote uniformity and consistency in the application of compensation mechanisms across different jurisdictions within India. This can contribute to fairer and more equitable compensation practices, reducing disparities and ensuring that workers receive appropriate compensation regardless of their location or jurisdiction.

Grievance Redressal Mechanisms:

1. Dispute Resolution Mechanisms: The Bharatiya Nyaya Sanhita, 2023's provisions on dispute resolution mechanisms, including alternative dispute resolution (ADR) methods such as mediation and arbitration, can have implications for the resolution of labour-related grievances. These mechanisms may provide more efficient and cost-effective means of resolving labour disputes, potentially reducing the time and resources required for traditional litigation.

2. Evidentiary Rules in Labour Disputes: The Bharatiya Sakshya, 2023's provisions on evidentiary rules can impact the way evidence is presented and evaluated in labour disputes. The code's guidelines on electronic evidence, expert testimony, and witness credibility can help ensure that labour disputes are resolved based on credible and admissible evidence, promoting fairness and transparency in the grievance redressal process.

3. Access to Legal Remedies: The consolidation and harmonization of civil laws under the Bharatiya Nyaya Sanhita, 2023, can potentially improve access to legal remedies for workers seeking redressal of their grievances. By streamlining and clarifying the legal framework, the code may facilitate a better understanding of available legal avenues and procedures, empowering workers to pursue their rights more effectively.

Overall, the implications of these three codes for worker safety, compensation, and grievance redressal mechanisms are multifaceted and far-reaching. While some provisions may directly enhance worker protection and compensation mechanisms, others may have indirect effects by influencing the legal framework, evidentiary rules, and dispute resolution processes. Employers, employees, trade unions, and policymakers will need to carefully analyze and interpret these implications to ensure the effective implementation of robust worker safety measures, fair compensation practices, and accessible grievance redressal mechanisms.

Changes in the Rules for Removal or Termination of Employees

The Bharatiya Nyaya Sanhita, 2023, also introduces notable changes to the rules governing the removal or termination of employees. These changes can have significant implications for both employers and employees, affecting job security, termination procedures, and the overall employment landscape in India.

1. Consolidation of Termination Provisions: The Bharatiya Nyaya Sanhita, 2023, aims to consolidate and harmonize the provisions related to the termination of employment across various labor laws. This consolidation can provide greater clarity and consistency in the application of termination rules, reducing ambiguities and potential conflicts arising from multiple sources of law.

2. Grounds for Termination: The code may introduce changes to the grounds for termination of employment, such as misconduct, poor performance, or operational requirements. These changes can impact the criteria and procedures that employers must follow when terminating an employee, potentially affecting job security and employee rights.

3. Procedural Safeguards: The Bharatiya Nyaya Sanhita, 2023, may establish procedural safeguards to ensure fairness and due process in termination proceedings. These safeguards may include provisions for adequate notice periods, opportunities for employees to respond or appeal, and mechanisms for resolving disputes related to termination.

4. Severance and Compensation: The code may introduce changes to the rules governing severance pay and compensation for terminated employees. These changes can impact the financial obligations of employers and the rights of employees to receive adequate compensation upon termination.

5. Retrenchment and Layoff Procedures: The Bharatiya Nyaya Sanhita, 2023, may address the procedures for retrenchment and layoffs, particularly in cases of organizational restructuring, economic downturns, or operational changes. These provisions can impact the rights of employees during mass terminations and the obligations of employers to follow fair and transparent processes.

6. Non-Compete and Non-Solicitation Clauses: The code's provisions on contract law may influence the interpretation and enforcement of non-compete and non-solicitation clauses in employment agreements. These clauses can impact an employee's ability to seek alternative employment or engage in certain business activities after termination.

7. Dispute Resolution Mechanisms: The Bharatiya Nyaya Sanhita, 2023, may introduce or modify dispute resolution mechanisms for termination-related disputes. These mechanisms, such as mediation, arbitration, or specialized labor tribunals, can impact the efficiency and fairness of resolving termination-related conflicts between employers and employees.

8. Evidentiary Standards: The Bharatiya Sakshya, 2023's provisions on evidentiary rules may influence the admissibility and evaluation of evidence in termination-related disputes. These provisions can impact the ability of employers and employees to present and substantiate their cases effectively, potentially affecting the outcomes of termination-related legal proceedings.

9. Public Interest Considerations: The Bharatiya Nyaya Sanhita, 2023, may incorporate provisions that balance the rights of

employers and employees with broader public interest considerations, such as economic growth, job creation, and industry competitiveness. These considerations can influence the formulation and application of termination rules.

10. Transitional Provisions and Future Amendments: The code may include transitional provisions to ensure a smooth transition from existing termination rules to the new framework. Additionally, provisions for periodic review and amendment can allow for adjustments and adaptations to the termination rules as economic, social, or legal conditions evolve.

The changes in the rules for removal or termination of employees introduced by the Bharatiya Nyaya Sanhita, 2023, have the potential to significantly impact the employment landscape in India. While these changes may aim to provide greater clarity and consistency, they may also necessitate adjustments for both employers and employees in terms of termination procedures, severance obligations, and dispute resolution mechanisms.

It is crucial for all stakeholders, including employers, employees, trade unions, and policymakers, to carefully analyze and interpret the implications of these changes. Effective implementation and compliance with the new termination rules can contribute to a more transparent and equitable employment environment, while balancing the rights and interests of both employers and employees.

As with any significant legal reform, the real-world impact of the changes in the rules for removal or termination of employees will become more apparent as cases are adjudicated and precedents are established. Ongoing monitoring, dialogue, and collaboration among stakeholders will be essential to address any emerging challenges or unintended consequences and to ensure the fair and effective application of the new termination rules.

Chapter 6:

Impact on Specific Labour Laws

The introduction of AI and automation in various industries has far-reaching consequences on labour laws and regulations. As technological advancements reshape the workforce, it becomes imperative to re-evaluate and adapt existing labour laws to address the emerging challenges and ensure the protection of workers' rights. This chapter delves into the impact of AI and automation on specific labour laws in India, analyzing how these technological disruptions necessitate revisions and updates to existing legal frameworks.

1. Industrial Disputes Act

The Industrial Disputes Act, 1947, is a pivotal piece of legislation aimed at regulating industrial relations and resolving disputes between employers and employees. With the advent of AI and automation, several aspects of this act may require reconsideration:

a. Definition of "Workman" and "Industry" The definitions of "workman" and "industry" in the act may need to be expanded to encompass workers involved in the development, deployment, and maintenance of AI systems and automated processes. This would ensure that these workers are afforded the same protections and rights as traditional workers.

b. Retrenchment and Layoffs As AI and automation displace certain job roles, the provisions related to retrenchment and layoffs may need to be reviewed. Clear guidelines and safeguards should be established to protect workers from arbitrary terminations and ensure fair compensation and retraining opportunities.

c. Dispute Resolution Mechanisms The dispute resolution mechanisms outlined in the act may require adaptation to address conflicts arising from the implementation of AI and automation technologies. Mechanisms for grievance redressal, mediation, and arbitration should be tailored to address the unique challenges posed by these technologies.

2. Minimum Wages Act

The Minimum Wages Act, 1948, aims to ensure fair and decent wages for workers across various industries. However, the introduction of AI and automation raises questions about the applicability of minimum wage laws to workers involved in these technologies:

a. Wage Determination The criteria for determining minimum wages may need to be revised to account for the skills and expertise required in AI and automation-related roles. Factors such as educational qualifications, technical proficiency, and the complexity of tasks should be considered.

b. Equal Pay for Equal Work The principle of "equal pay for equal work" enshrined in the act may require clarification in the context of AI and automation. Clear guidelines should be established to ensure that workers performing similar tasks, whether augmented by AI or not, receive fair and equitable remuneration.

c. Skill Development and Upskilling Provisions for skill development and upskilling programs may need to be incorporated into the act to facilitate the transition of workers into AI and automation-related roles. This would help mitigate the potential displacement of workers and promote their employability in the changing landscape.

3. Contract Labour (Regulation and Abolition) Act

The Contract Labour (Regulation and Abolition) Act, 1970, regulates the employment of contract labour and aims to abolish the system in specific circumstances. The impact of AI and automation on this act may include:

a. Definition of "Contract Labour" The definition of "contract labour" may need to be expanded to include workers engaged in the development, deployment, and maintenance of AI systems and automated processes, whether employed directly or through third-party contractors.

b. Regulation of AI and Automation Service Providers Specific provisions may be required to regulate the activities of AI and automation service providers, ensuring they adhere to labour standards, provide adequate training, and uphold workers' rights.

c. Abolition of Contract Labour The criteria for determining the abolition of contract labour may need to be revisited in the context of AI and automation. Clear guidelines should be established to identify situations where the use of AI or automation may necessitate the abolition of contract labour in certain industries or processes.

4. Equal Remuneration Act

The Equal Remuneration Act, 1976, aims to prevent discrimination in remuneration based on gender. With the advent of AI and automation, the following aspects may require attention:

a. Non-discriminatory Algorithms Measures should be taken to ensure that AI algorithms and automated decision-making processes used in recruitment, performance evaluation, and remuneration are free from gender bias and discrimination.

b. Equal Pay for AI-Augmented Work Guidelines should be established to ensure that workers performing similar tasks, whether augmented by AI or not, receive equal remuneration, regardless of gender.

c. Skill Development and Upskilling Provisions for skill development and upskilling programs should be gender-neutral, providing equal opportunities for men and women to transition into AI and automation-related roles.

5. Other Labour Laws

The impact of AI and automation extends beyond the specific laws mentioned above. Several other labour laws and regulations may require review and adaptation, including:

a. Occupational Safety and Health Laws As AI and automation introduce new work environments and processes, occupational safety and health laws may need to be updated to address potential risks and hazards associated with these technologies.

b. Labour Welfare Laws Existing labour welfare laws, such as the Employees' State Insurance Act and the Employees' Provident Funds and Miscellaneous Provisions Act, may need to be revised to ensure appropriate social security and welfare benefits for workers affected by AI and automation.

c. Employment Exchange Laws Laws governing employment exchanges and job placement services may require updates to facilitate the matching of workers with AI and automation-related job opportunities, as well as the provision of necessary training and skill development programs.

d. Labour Inspection and Enforcement Mechanisms for labour inspection and enforcement may need to be strengthened to ensure compliance with updated labour laws and regulations related to AI and automation. Inspectors and enforcement officials may require specialized training to effectively monitor and address potential violations.

In conclusion, the impact of AI and automation on labour laws is multifaceted and far-reaching. Existing legal frameworks must be carefully examined and adapted to address the evolving nature of work, protect workers' rights, and promote fair and equitable employment practices in the age of technological disruption. Collaborative efforts between policymakers, legal experts, industry representatives, and worker organizations are crucial to ensure a smooth transition and the creation of a regulatory environment that strikes a balance between technological progress and the safeguarding of labour rights and welfare.

Chapter 7:

Case Studies and Practical Implications

The enactment of the Bharatiya Nyay Sanhita, 2023 (Indian Code of Laws), the Bharatiya Sakshya, 2023 (Indian Evidence Act), and the Bharatiya Nagarik Suraksha Sanhita, 2023 (Indian Civil Protection Code) represents a seismic shift in India's legal landscape. These comprehensive codes, aimed at modernizing and consolidating various areas of law, have far-reaching implications for individuals, businesses, and society as a whole. To better understand the practical impact of these landmark legislations, it is instructive to examine real-world case studies and explore the practical implications for key stakeholders in the realm of labour and employment.

Case Study 1: The Workplace Safety Incident

Background: Acme Manufacturing Ltd., a leading automotive parts manufacturer, faced a devastating incident at one of its production facilities. A series of explosions occurred in the chemical storage area, resulting in severe injuries to several workers and significant structural damage to the plant. Investigations revealed that the incident was caused by a combination of outdated safety protocols, inadequate training, and a lack of proper maintenance and inspections.

Impact of the New Codes: The Bharatiya Nyaya Sanhita, 2023, and the Bharatiya Nagarik Suraksha Sanhita, 2023, played a pivotal role in addressing the legal and regulatory aspects of this workplace safety incident.

Under the Bharatiya Nyaya Sanhita, 2023, Acme Manufacturing Ltd. faced potential liabilities under the provisions of tort law. The code's comprehensive treatment of negligence, strict liability, and duty of care principles provided a robust legal framework for establishing liability and determining appropriate compensation for the affected workers and their families.

Furthermore, the Bharatiya Nagarik Suraksha Sanhita, 2023, introduced stringent regulations for emergency preparedness and worker safety. Acme Manufacturing Ltd. was required to comply with the code's provisions on risk assessments, emergency response plans, and workplace disaster preparedness measures. Failure to adhere to these regulations could result in significant penalties and legal consequences.

7.1 Practical Implications:

1. Employers: This case study underscores the importance of prioritizing workplace safety and fostering a culture of compliance within organizations. Employers must ensure that their safety protocols, training programs, and maintenance procedures are up-to-date and aligned with the latest industry standards and legal requirements. Conducting regular risk assessments, investing in employee training, and implementing robust emergency response plans are crucial steps to mitigate potential liabilities and protect the well-being of workers.

2. Employees: The new codes empower employees by providing a stronger legal framework for seeking redress in cases of workplace injuries or safety violations. Employees should be aware of their rights and responsibilities under the new laws, and actively participate in safety training programs and reporting mechanisms. Additionally, employees can play a crucial role in promoting a culture of safety within their workplaces by adhering

to established protocols and reporting any potential hazards or concerns to management.

3. Labour Unions: Labour unions have a significant role to play in advocating for safer working conditions and ensuring that employers comply with the provisions of the new codes. Unions can collaborate with employers to develop comprehensive safety policies, monitor compliance, and represent the interests of workers in legal proceedings or negotiations related to workplace safety incidents.

Case Study 2: The Gig Economy Dispute

Background: Rideshare Inc., a prominent ride-hailing platform, faced a legal challenge from a group of its drivers who claimed to be misclassified as independent contractors rather than employees. The drivers alleged that they were entitled to various benefits and protections under labour laws, including minimum wage, overtime pay, and access to social security schemes.

Rideshare Inc. is one of the largest and most recognizable ride-hailing platforms globally, operating in hundreds of cities across multiple countries. The company's business model relies on a vast network of independent contractors, referred to as "driver-partners," who use their personal vehicles to provide transportation services to customers through the Rideshare app.

The controversy surrounding the classification of Rideshare drivers as independent contractors or employees has been a long-standing and contentious issue, not just for Rideshare Inc. but for the entire gig economy. The distinction between these two categories carries significant implications for workers' rights, benefits, and the obligations of companies toward their workforce.

The Legal Challenge

In early 2021, a group of Rideshare drivers, represented by a prominent labor law firm, filed a class-action lawsuit against the company, alleging that they were misclassified as independent contractors when they should have been classified as employees under applicable labor laws.

The plaintiffs argued that Rideshare exercised a significant degree of control over their work, dictating various aspects of their job, such as setting fares, determining service areas, and enforcing strict performance standards. They claimed that this level of control, coupled with the integral role they played in Rideshare's core business operations, effectively made them employees rather than independent contractors.

The drivers sought various remedies, including:

1. Minimum wage and overtime pay: The plaintiffs argued that by classifying them as independent contractors, Rideshare had deprived them of their right to receive minimum wage and overtime compensation as required by federal and state labor laws.

2. Access to employee benefits: The drivers contended that they should have been eligible for benefits typically provided to employees, such as health insurance, paid time off, and contributions to social security and unemployment insurance programs.

3. Reimbursement of expenses: The plaintiffs sought reimbursement for expenses incurred while working for Rideshare, including

vehicle maintenance, fuel costs, and other job-related expenses, which are typically covered by employers for their employees.

4. Statutory penalties and interest: The drivers sought to recover statutory penalties and interest for Rideshare's alleged violations of labor laws, including failure to provide wage statements, pay stubs, and other required documentation.

Rideshare's Defense

In response to the lawsuit, Rideshare vehemently defended its classification of drivers as independent contractors. The company argued that its platform was designed to provide flexibility and autonomy to its driver-partners, allowing them to choose when, where, and how much they wanted to work.

Rideshare's legal team contended that the drivers were not subject to the level of control typically associated with an employer-employee relationship. They highlighted the following points:

1. Flexible scheduling: Drivers were free to log in and out of the Rideshare app at their convenience, without any mandatory shifts or work schedules imposed by the company.

2. No direct supervision: Rideshare did not directly supervise or manage the drivers' work, nor did it provide training or instructions on how to perform their duties.

3. Use of personal assets: Drivers used their personal vehicles and were responsible for maintaining and insuring them, which is characteristic of independent contractors operating their own businesses.

4. Ability to work for competitors: Drivers were free to work for other ride-hailing platforms or pursue other income-generating

opportunities simultaneously, which is inconsistent with the exclusive nature of an employer-employee relationship.

Rideshare also argued that classifying drivers as employees would fundamentally undermine the flexibility and autonomy that attracted many individuals to the gig economy in the first place. The company maintained that its business model relied on the independent contractor classification and that changing this status would impose significant operational and financial burdens, potentially leading to higher costs for consumers and fewer work opportunities for drivers.

Legal Precedents and Regulatory Landscape

The legal battle between Rideshare and its drivers unfolded against a backdrop of evolving legal precedents and regulatory efforts to address the challenges posed by the gig economy.

In various jurisdictions, courts have issued conflicting rulings on the classification of gig workers, with some favoring the employee status and others upholding the independent contractor model. These divergent rulings have highlighted the need for clearer and more consistent guidelines to address the unique characteristics of the gig economy.

Governments and regulatory bodies have also grappled with the issue, exploring legislative and regulatory solutions to strike a balance between protecting workers' rights and fostering innovation in the gig economy. Some jurisdictions have proposed creating a new category of "dependent contractors" or "gig workers" with a hybrid status, entitled to certain benefits and protections while maintaining some degree of flexibility.

The Rideshare case was closely watched by other gig economy companies, labor advocates, and policymakers, as its outcome could have far-reaching implications for the industry and potentially shape future regulations and legal precedents.

Public Perception and Societal Impact

Beyond the legal and regulatory implications, the Rideshare case also sparked broader discussions about the societal impact of the gig economy and the changing nature of work in the 21st century.

Proponents of the independent contractor model argued that it provided opportunities for flexible work arrangements, allowing individuals to supplement their income or transition between careers. They contended that the gig economy empowered workers and fostered entrepreneurship.

Critics, however, raised concerns about the precarious nature of gig work, the lack of job security, and the potential for exploitation of workers without adequate protections. They argued that the classification of workers as independent contractors was often a means for companies to avoid their obligations and shift risks onto individual workers.

The case also highlighted issues of economic inequality and the growing divide between those with stable, well-compensated jobs and those engaged in precarious, low-wage gig work. Some labor advocates and policymakers called for stronger social safety nets and worker protections to address these disparities and ensure a more equitable distribution of the benefits of the gig economy.

As the legal battle unfolded, public opinion remained divided, with some supporting Rideshare's position as a means of preserving the flexibility and innovation of the gig economy, while others sided with the drivers, advocating for greater workers' rights and protections.

The legal challenge faced by Rideshare Inc. regarding the classification of its drivers as independent contractors or employees was a complex and multifaceted issue with far-reaching implications. It exposed the tensions between traditional labour laws and the evolving realities of the gig economy, highlighting the need for legal and regulatory frameworks to adapt to the changing nature of work.

Regardless of the outcome, the case sparked important conversations about workers' rights, the future of employment relationships, and the societal impact of the gig economy. As technological advancements continue to disrupt traditional business models, it is likely that similar legal battles and policy discussions will persist, shaping the future of work and the protections afforded to workers in the years to come.

Impact of the New Codes: The Bharatiya Nyaya Sanhita, 2023, played a crucial role in addressing the legal complexities surrounding the gig economy and the classification of workers.

The code's provisions on contract law provided a framework for examining the nature of the agreement between Rideshare Inc. and its drivers. The code's principles of offer, acceptance, consideration, and intention helped determine whether the drivers were truly independent contractors or whether their arrangement with the company constituted an employment relationship.

Additionally, the Bharatiya Nyaya Sanhita, 2023, incorporated provisions for addressing emerging employment models and protecting the rights of workers in non-traditional arrangements. These provisions aimed to strike a balance between the flexibility of the gig economy and ensuring fair treatment and access to basic protections for workers.

Implications

1. Employers: Companies operating in the gig economy must carefully review their employment models and contractual arrangements with workers in light of the legal developments and potential regulatory changes.

a. Compliance and Risk Assessment:

Companies like Rideshare Inc. need to conduct a thorough review of their current practices and policies to ensure compliance with applicable labor laws and regulations. They should seek legal counsel to assess the risk of misclassifying workers as independent contractors and potential exposure to liabilities, such as back pay, penalties, and other legal consequences.

b. Employment Models and Contractual Arrangements:

Depending on the outcome of the Rideshare case and potential regulatory changes, companies may need to reevaluate their employment models and contractual arrangements with workers. They may need to consider reclassifying certain categories of workers as employees, or explore alternative arrangements that provide greater flexibility while still complying with labor laws.

c. Cost and Operational Impact:

If companies are required to reclassify significant portions of their workforce as employees, they must prepare for the associated costs and operational changes. This may include providing employee benefits, such as health insurance, paid time off, and retirement contributions, as well as adjusting compensation structures to comply with minimum wage and overtime regulations. Companies should conduct financial modeling and scenario planning to understand the potential impact on their business models and profitability.

d. Worker Management and Supervision:

If workers are classified as employees, companies may need to implement more structured management and supervision practices. This could include providing training, setting work schedules, monitoring performance, and exercising greater control over the work process. Companies should assess their readiness for these changes and develop strategies to maintain operational efficiency while complying with employment laws.

2. Employees/Workers: The new legal landscape surrounding the gig economy provides greater clarity and protection for workers in non-traditional employment arrangements.

a. Understanding Rights and Entitlements:

Gig workers should familiarize themselves with their rights and entitlements under the new laws and regulations. This may include the right to minimum wage, overtime pay, access to employee benefits, and protection against discrimination and unfair labor practices. Workers should stay informed about the legal developments and seek guidance from labor organizations or legal professionals if they have concerns about their employment status or treatment.

b. Seeking Redress for Misclassification:

If workers believe they have been misclassified as independent contractors when they should be classified as employees, they may have legal recourse to challenge their employment status. Workers can file complaints with relevant labor authorities, seek legal representation, or join class-action lawsuits to assert their rights and seek remedies for unpaid wages, benefits, and other entitlements.

c. Negotiating Better Terms and Conditions:

With greater legal protections and recognition of their employment status, gig workers may have more leverage to negotiate better terms and conditions with their employers. This could include higher pay rates, access to benefits, reimbursement for job-related expenses, and improved grievance procedures.

d. Collective Bargaining and Unionization:

The legal developments surrounding the gig economy may also open up opportunities for gig workers to engage in collective bargaining and unionization efforts. By forming or joining unions, workers can collectively advocate for their rights, negotiate better terms and conditions, and have a more powerful voice in shaping the policies and practices of their employers.

3. Labor Unions: Labor unions have an opportunity to extend their reach and advocacy efforts to the growing gig economy workforce.

a. Outreach and Engagement:

Labor unions should actively reach out to gig workers and understand their unique challenges, concerns, and aspirations. By building relationships and trust with this workforce, unions can better represent their interests and tailor their advocacy efforts to address the specific needs of the gig economy.

b. Organizing and Collective Bargaining:

Unions can play a pivotal role in organizing gig workers, facilitating collective bargaining efforts, and negotiating better terms and conditions with employers. This may involve adapting traditional union models to accommodate the flexible nature of gig work or exploring new organizing strategies tailored to the gig economy.

c. Legal and Policy Advocacy:

Labor unions can leverage their expertise and resources to advocate for legal and policy changes that protect the rights of gig workers. This could involve lobbying for legislation that clarifies the employment status of gig workers, establishes industry-specific standards, or creates new categories of worker classification with appropriate protections and benefits.

d. Collaboration and Partnerships:

Unions can collaborate with other stakeholders, such as worker advocacy groups, legal organizations, and policymakers, to form coalitions and partnerships that amplify their voices and efforts. By working together, they can push for comprehensive solutions that address the challenges faced by gig workers and shape the future of work in the gig economy.

4. Regulatory Bodies and Policymakers:

a. Clarifying Legal Definitions and Criteria:

Regulatory bodies and policymakers must address the ambiguities and inconsistencies in the legal definitions and criteria used to classify workers as employees or independent contractors. They should work towards developing clear and consistent guidelines that take into account the unique characteristics of the gig economy while ensuring fair treatment and protections for workers.

b. Updating Labor Laws and Regulations:

Labor laws and regulations may need to be updated or amended to address the challenges posed by the gig economy. This could involve creating new categories of worker classification, such as "dependent contractors" or "gig workers," with specific rights and protections tailored to their employment arrangement. Policymakers should consider input from all stakeholders, including employers, workers, and labor organizations, to develop balanced and effective regulations.

c. Enforcement and Oversight:

Robust enforcement mechanisms and oversight processes should be established to ensure compliance with labor laws and regulations in the gig economy. This may involve empowering labor authorities with the necessary resources and tools to conduct investigations, impose penalties for violations, and provide effective remedies for workers who have been mistreated or misclassified.

d. Promoting Fair Competition and Innovation:

While ensuring worker protections, policymakers should also consider the need to promote fair competition and innovation within the gig economy. This could involve exploring incentives or regulatory frameworks that encourage responsible business practices, foster innovation, and create a level playing field for companies that properly classify and compensate their workers.

5. Public Awareness and Education:

a. Raising Awareness about Worker Rights and Protections:

There is a need for increased public awareness and education about the rights and protections afforded to gig workers under the new legal and regulatory frameworks. Public campaigns, informational resources, and community outreach efforts can help workers understand their entitlements and empower them to assert their rights.

b. Addressing Misconceptions and Stigma:

Efforts should be made to address any misconceptions or stigma surrounding gig work and the employment status of gig workers. By promoting a better understanding of the realities and challenges faced by this workforce, society can foster greater empathy, support, and advocacy for their fair treatment and inclusion in labor protection frameworks.

c. Encouraging Responsible Business Practices:

Public awareness initiatives can also target businesses and employers, encouraging them to adopt responsible and ethical practices in their treatment of gig workers. This could involve highlighting the benefits of fair labor practices, such as improved worker loyalty, productivity, and overall business sustainability.

d. Fostering Dialogue and Collaboration:

Public forums, panel discussions, and other platforms can be created to facilitate dialogue and collaboration among various stakeholders, including workers, employers, labor organizations, policymakers, and academic institutions. By promoting open and constructive discourse, innovative solutions and best practices can emerge to address the challenges of the gig economy and foster a more equitable and sustainable future of work.

In conclusion, the legal challenge faced by Rideshare Inc. and the evolving regulatory landscape surrounding the gig economy have far-reaching practical implications for employers, workers, labor unions, policymakers, and society as a whole. It highlights the need for a comprehensive and collaborative approach to address the complexities of the gig economy, ensure fair treatment and protections for workers, while also promoting innovation and responsible business practices. By addressing these practical implications proactively and collaboratively, stakeholders can shape a future of work that balances the interests of all parties and creates a more equitable and sustainable gig economy.

Case Study 3: The Cross-Border Employment Dispute

Background: GlobalTech Solutions, a multinational technology company, faced a legal challenge from a group of Indian employees working at its subsidiary in Singapore. The employees claimed that they were subjected to discriminatory practices, including unequal pay and promotion opportunities compared to their Singaporean counterparts. They sought redress under Indian labour laws, citing their Indian citizenship and the company's Indian parent entity.

Impact of the New Codes: The Bharatiya Nyaya Sanhita, 2023, and the Bharatiya Sakshya, 2023, played crucial roles in addressing the legal complexities of this cross-border employment dispute.

The Bharatiya Nyaya Sanhita, 2023, and the Bharatiya Sakshya, 2023, represent landmark legal developments in India, designed to address the complexities of cross-border employment relationships and modernize the rules of evidence in legal proceedings. These laws aim to provide a comprehensive framework for resolving disputes and ensuring fair treatment of employees, regardless of their geographical location, while also facilitating the admissibility and evaluation of various forms of evidence in legal proceedings.

The Bharatiya Nyaya Sanhita, 2023, tackles the intricate issues that arise when employment relationships transcend national boundaries. In an increasingly globalized world, where multinational companies and their subsidiaries operate across multiple jurisdictions, the need for a clear legal framework to govern these cross-border relationships has become paramount.

One of the key provisions of the Bharatiya Nyaya Sanhita, 2023, is the guidance it provides on the applicability of Indian labour laws to employees working for Indian companies or their subsidiaries abroad. This law recognizes that employment relationships in such scenarios can be complex, with various factors influencing the applicable legal framework.

The Bharatiya Nyaya Sanhita, 2023, takes into account several factors when determining the applicability of Indian labour laws, including the place of employment, the governing laws specified in the employment contracts, and the principles of non-discrimination and equal treatment. By considering these factors, the law aims to strike a balance between protecting the rights of employees and providing a conducive environment for businesses to operate in a globalized world.

For instance, if an Indian employee is working for an Indian company or its subsidiary abroad, the Bharatiya Nyaya Sanhita, 2023, may deem Indian labour laws applicable, provided that certain conditions are met. These conditions could include the employee's primary place of work being within India, or the employment contract explicitly specifying the applicability of Indian labour laws.

However, the law also recognizes that there may be instances where the application of Indian labour laws may not be appropriate or feasible, such as when the employment relationship is governed by the laws of the host country or when the principles of non-discrimination and equal treatment dictate the application of the host country's laws.

By addressing these cross-border employment relationships, the Bharatiya Nyaya Sanhita, 2023, aims to provide a level playing field for employees, ensuring that their rights are protected and that they are not subjected to unfair treatment based on their location or nationality. This is particularly important in the era of globalization, where multinational companies and their subsidiaries operate across multiple jurisdictions, and employees may find themselves navigating complex legal landscapes.

Furthermore, the Bharatiya Sakshya, 2023, introduces modernized rules of evidence that facilitate the admissibility and evaluation of various forms of evidence in legal proceedings. This law recognizes the evolving nature of evidence and the increasing reliance on electronic records, witness testimonies, and expert opinions in legal disputes.

In today's digital age, where a significant portion of evidence exists in electronic form, such as emails, text messages, and digital documents, the Bharatiya Sakshya, 2023, provides a framework for admitting and evaluating such evidence in legal proceedings. This is particularly relevant in cross-border disputes, where evidence may be scattered across multiple jurisdictions and presented in various formats.

The Bharatiya Sakshya, 2023, also addresses the admissibility and evaluation of witness testimonies and expert opinions, which can be crucial in resolving complex legal disputes. In cross-border cases, where witnesses or experts may be located in different countries, the law provides guidance on how their testimonies and opinions can be presented and considered as evidence.

By modernizing the rules of evidence, the Bharatiya Sakshya, 2023, aims to ensure that legal proceedings are conducted in a fair and efficient manner, taking into account the realities of the digital age and the complexities of cross-border disputes.

The practical implications of these legal developments are far-reaching and encompass various stakeholders, including employers, employees, and labour unions. Multinational companies and those with cross-border operations must remain vigilant in ensuring compliance with the labour laws and regulations of the countries in which they operate, as well as the provisions of the Bharatiya Nyay Sanhita, 2023.

Employers should review their employment contracts, policies, and practices to ensure adherence to principles of non-discrimination and equal treatment, regardless of the geographical location of their employees. This may involve revising employment contracts to clearly specify the applicable labour laws, updating policies to reflect the provisions of the Bharatiya Nyaya Sanhita, 2023, and providing training to human resources personnel and managers to ensure consistent implementation of these policies across all locations.

On the other hand, employees working for Indian companies abroad now have a legal framework to seek redress and assert their rights under Indian labour laws, subject to certain conditions and factors. Employees should be aware of their rights and obligations under the new codes and seek legal counsel if they believe they have been subjected to discriminatory or unfair practices by their employers.

Labour unions can also play a crucial role in advocating for the rights of Indian workers employed by multinational companies or their subsidiaries abroad. By collaborating with international counterparts and leveraging the provisions of the new codes, unions can represent the interests of these workers and ensure fair treatment and adherence to labour standards across borders.

Unions can engage in collective bargaining with multinational employers, advocating for the inclusion of provisions that align with the principles of the Bharatiya Nyaya Sanhita, 2023, such as non-discrimination and equal treatment. They can also provide legal assistance and support to individual employees who may be facing disputes or challenges related to their cross-border employment relationships.

Additionally, the modernized rules of evidence introduced by the Bharatiya Sakshya, 2023, have implications for legal professionals, such as lawyers, judges, and expert witnesses. These stakeholders must familiarize themselves with the new rules and develop strategies for effectively presenting and evaluating various forms of evidence in legal proceedings.

Lawyers may need to adapt their trial strategies and techniques to effectively utilize electronic records, witness testimonies, and expert opinions as evidence. They may also need to collaborate with technical experts or consultants to ensure proper handling and presentation of digital evidence.

Judges and other legal authorities will need to be trained in the application of the new rules of evidence, ensuring that they are equipped to make informed decisions regarding the admissibility and evaluation of various types of evidence in legal proceedings.

Expert witnesses, such as forensic analysts, digital experts, or subject matter specialists, may play an increasingly important role in cross-border disputes, where their expertise may be required to interpret and analyze complex forms of evidence.

Furthermore, the implementation of these new laws may necessitate the development of specialized legal infrastructures and resources, such as dedicated courts or tribunals for handling cross-border employment disputes, as well as the establishment of centralized databases or repositories for storing and managing cross-border evidence.

Overall, the Bharatiya Nyaya Sanhita, 2023, and the Bharatiya Sakshya, 2023, represent significant strides in addressing the complexities of cross-border employment relationships and evidentiary rules in India. These laws aim to strike a balance between protecting the rights of employees and providing a conducive environment for businesses to operate in a globalized world, while also ensuring that legal proceedings are conducted in a fair and efficient manner.

However, the effective implementation and enforcement of these laws will be crucial in ensuring that their intended objectives are achieved. Collaboration and coordination among various stakeholders, including government authorities, employers, employees, labour unions, and legal professionals, will be essential to navigate the complexities and challenges that may arise.

Continuous monitoring, evaluation, and refinement of these laws may be necessary to address emerging issues and adapt to the ever-evolving landscape of cross-border employment and legal proceedings. Additionally, promoting awareness and education about these new laws among all stakeholders will be vital to ensure their widespread adoption and impact.

Ultimately, the Bharatiya Nyaya Sanhita, 2023, and the Bharatiya Sakshya, 2023, represent India's commitment to fostering a fair and equitable legal environment that keeps pace with the demands of a globalized world, while upholding the principles of justice, fairness, and the rule of law.

Case Study 4: The Whistleblower Retaliation Case

Background: Deepa Singh, an employee at a prominent pharmaceutical company, uncovered evidence of unethical marketing practices and potential violations of consumer protection laws. She reported these concerns through the company's internal whistleblower channels. However, instead of addressing her allegations, the company terminated her employment, citing "performance issues" as the reason.

Impact of the New Codes: The Bharatiya Nyaya Sanhita, 2023, played a crucial role in providing legal protection to whistleblowers like Deepa Singh. The code incorporated provisions that safeguarded the rights of employees who report unethical or illegal activities within their organizations, shielding them from retaliation, such as termination, demotion, or harassment.

Additionally, the code's provisions on evidentiary rules, as outlined in the Bharatiya Sakshya, 2023, facilitated the admissibility and evaluation of various forms of evidence, including electronic communications, internal records, and witness testimonies, which were crucial in substantiating Deepa's allegations and establishing a case of wrongful termination.

Practical Implications:

1. Employers: Organizations must establish robust whistleblower protection policies and mechanisms that align with the provisions of the Bharatiya Nyaya Sanhita, 2023. Employers should foster a culture of transparency and ethical conduct, where employees feel empowered to raise concerns without fear of retaliation. Thorough investigations and appropriate remedial actions should be taken in response to whistleblower reports.

2. Employees: The new codes empower employees to report unethical or illegal practices without the fear of reprisal. Employees should familiarize themselves with their organization's whistleblower policies and the legal protections afforded by the Bharatiya Nyaya Sanhita, 2023. They should also maintain detailed documentation and records to support their allegations, as these may be crucial in legal proceedings.

3. Labour Unions: Labour unions can play a vital role in advocating for whistleblower rights and ensuring that employers adhere to the provisions of the new codes. Unions can provide guidance, support, and legal representation to employees who face retaliation for reporting misconduct, leveraging the protections enshrined in the Bharatiya Nyaya Sanhita, 2023.

Case Study 5: The Equal Pay Dispute

Background: At a renowned technology firm, a group of female software engineers discovered a significant pay disparity between themselves and their male counterparts, despite having similar qualifications, experience, and job responsibilities. They filed a complaint alleging gender-based discrimination in compensation practices, citing violations of labour laws and the principles of equal pay for equal work.

Impact of the New Codes: The Bharatiya Nyaya Sanhita, 2023, played a pivotal role in addressing this equal pay dispute. The code's provisions on non-discrimination and equal treatment in employment were instrumental in establishing the legal grounds for the female engineers' claims. The code reinforced the principles of equal pay for equal work, prohibiting discrimination based on gender or any other protected characteristics.

Furthermore, the Bharatiya Sakshya, 2023, facilitated the admissibility and evaluation of evidence crucial to substantiating the pay disparity allegations. This included payroll records, performance evaluations, and statistical analyses demonstrating the gender-based pay gap within the organization.

Practical Implications:

1. Employers: Organizations must conduct regular pay equity audits and ensure that their compensation practices are free from discrimination based on gender or any other protected characteristics. Employers should implement transparent and objective criteria for determining salaries, promotions, and bonuses, aligning their policies and practices with the principles of equal pay for equal work enshrined in the Bharatiya Nyaya Sanhita, 2023.

2. Employees: The new codes empower employees to challenge discriminatory compensation practices and assert their rights to equal pay for equal work. Employees should be vigilant in identifying potential pay disparities and gather relevant evidence, such as pay stubs, performance reviews, and job descriptions, to support their claims.

3. Labour Unions: Labour unions can play a crucial role in advocating for pay equity and challenging discriminatory compensation practices. They can leverage the provisions of the Bharatiya Nyaya Sanhita, 2023, to negotiate fair and equitable pay scales, conduct wage audits, and represent employees in legal proceedings related to equal pay disputes.

Case Study 6: The Workplace Harassment Case

Background: At a prominent advertising agency, multiple employees reported instances of severe and persistent workplace harassment by a senior executive. The harassment included verbal abuse, inappropriate comments, and unwanted physical contact. Despite repeated complaints, the agency failed to take adequate action, citing the executive's influential position and contributions to the company.

Impact of the New Codes: The Bharatiya Nyaya Sanhita, 2023, played a crucial role in addressing this workplace harassment case. The code's provisions on sexual harassment, discrimination, and workplace conduct established clear guidelines and legal obligations for employers to maintain a safe and respectful work environment free from harassment and abuse.

Furthermore, the Bharatiya Sakshya, 2023, facilitated the admissibility and evaluation of various forms of evidence in support of the employees' claims. This included witness testimonies, contemporaneous documentation of incidents, and expert opinions on the psychological impact of workplace harassment.

Practical Implications:

1. Employers: Organizations must implement robust anti-harassment policies and procedures that align with the provisions of the Bharatiya Nyaya Sanhita, 2023. This includes establishing clear reporting mechanisms, conducting thorough investigations, and taking appropriate disciplinary action in response to substantiated claims of harassment or abuse. Employers must foster a culture of respect and zero-tolerance for any form of harassment or discrimination in the workplace.

2. Employees: The new codes empower employees to report instances of workplace harassment without fear of retaliation or discrimination. Employees should familiarize themselves with their organization's anti-harassment policies and the legal protections afforded by the Bharatiya Nyaya Sanhita, 2023. They should maintain detailed records and documentation to support their claims, and seek assistance from relevant authorities or legal counsel if necessary.

3. Labour Unions: Labour unions can play a vital role in advocating for safe and respectful work environments. They can collaborate with employers to develop and implement effective anti-harassment policies, provide support and representation to employees who have experienced harassment, and ensure that employers adhere to the provisions of the Bharatiya Nyaya Sanhita, 2023.

Case Study 7: The Industrial Accident Compensation Case

Background: In a tragic incident at a construction site, a scaffolding collapse resulted in severe injuries to several workers. The injured workers and their families filed claims for compensation and medical expenses, alleging that the construction company had failed to implement adequate safety measures and provide proper training to its employees.

Impact of the New Codes: The Bharatiya Nyaya Sanhita, 2023, played a pivotal role in determining liability and compensation in this industrial accident case. The code's provisions on tort law, including negligence and strict liability, provided a framework for establishing the construction company's legal obligations and potential culpability for the incident.

Additionally, the Bharatiya Sakshya, 2023, facilitated the admissibility and evaluation of various forms of evidence, such as expert testimonies, safety inspection reports, and witness accounts, which were crucial in substantiating the workers' claims and demonstrating the company's failure to comply with safety protocols.

Practical Implications:

1. Employers: Organizations operating in high-risk industries, such as construction, must prioritize workplace safety and comply with relevant safety regulations and industry best practices. Employers should implement comprehensive safety training programs, conduct regular risk assessments, and ensure that adequate safety measures are in place to protect their employees. Failure to do so can result in significant legal liabilities and compensation claims under the provisions of the Bharatiya Nyaya Sanhita, 2023.

2. Employees: The new codes empower employees and their families to seek compensation and legal redress in cases of industrial accidents or occupational injuries. Employees should be aware of their rights and legal protections under the Bharatiya Nyaya Sanhita, 2023, and maintain detailed records and documentation related to workplace safety incidents.

3. Labour Unions: Labour unions can play a crucial role in advocating for improved workplace safety standards and holding employers accountable for violations. They can collaborate with employers to develop and implement comprehensive safety programs, conduct independent safety audits, and represent workers in legal proceedings related to industrial accidents and compensation claims.

Case Study 8: The Data Privacy and Employee Monitoring Dispute

Background: A leading technology firm faced allegations of excessive and intrusive employee monitoring practices, including the collection and analysis of employee communications, browsing history, and productivity data without proper consent or transparency. Employees raised concerns about violations of privacy and potential misuse of their personal data.

Impact of the New Codes: The Bharatiya Nyaya Sanhita, 2023, played a crucial role in addressing this data privacy and employee monitoring dispute. The code's provisions on privacy rights, data protection, and fair information practices established legal boundaries for employers' data collection and monitoring activities, ensuring respect for employees' privacy and personal autonomy.

Additionally, the Bharatiya Sakshya, 2023, facilitated the admissibility and evaluation of electronic evidence and expert testimonies related to the company's data collection practices, enabling a thorough examination of the extent and appropriateness of the monitoring activities.

Practical Implications:

1. Employers: Organizations must develop and implement comprehensive data privacy and employee monitoring policies that align with the provisions of the Bharatiya Nyaya Sanhita, 2023. These policies should strike a balance between legitimate business interests and employees' reasonable expectations of privacy. Employers should obtain informed consent, provide transparency about data collection practices, and limit monitoring activities to what is strictly necessary and proportionate.

2. Employees: The new codes empower employees to assert their privacy rights and challenge excessive or intrusive monitoring

practices by their employers. Employees should familiarize themselves with their organization's data privacy policies and the legal protections afforded by the Bharatiya Nyaya Sanhita, 2023. They should also be vigilant about providing consent for data collection and monitoring activities.

3. Labour Unions: Labour unions can play a vital role in advocating for employee privacy rights and negotiating fair and transparent data privacy policies with employers. They can provide guidance and representation to employees who believe their privacy rights have been violated, leveraging the provisions of the Bharatiya Nyaya Sanhita, 2023.

Case Study 9: The Gig Worker Misclassification Dispute

Background: A prominent food delivery platform faced a legal challenge from a group of its delivery personnel, who claimed that they had been misclassified as independent contractors rather than employees. The workers alleged that they were entitled to various benefits and protections under labour laws, including minimum wage, overtime pay, and access to social security schemes.

Impact of the New Codes: The Bharatiya Nyaya Sanhita, 2023, played a crucial role in addressing this gig worker misclassification dispute. The code's provisions on employment contracts and worker classification provided a framework for examining the nature of the relationship between the food delivery platform and its delivery personnel.

The code's principles of offer, acceptance, consideration, and intention were instrumental in determining whether the delivery workers were truly independent contractors or whether their arrangement with the platform constituted an employment relationship, entitling them to the protections and benefits of labour laws.

Furthermore, the Bharatiya Sakshya, 2023, facilitated the admissibility and evaluation of various forms of evidence, such as employment agreements, work schedules, and payment records, which were crucial in substantiating the workers' claims and establishing the true nature of their relationship with the platform.

Practical Implications:

1. Employers: Companies operating in the gig economy must carefully review their employment models and contractual arrangements with workers in light of the provisions of the Bharatiya Nyaya Sanhita, 2023. Misclassifying workers as independent contractors to circumvent labour laws and obligations can result in significant legal and financial consequences. Employers should seek legal counsel to ensure compliance with the code's provisions and adapt their practices accordingly.

2. Workers: The new codes empower gig workers to challenge their misclassification and assert their rights to employment benefits and protections. Workers should familiarize themselves with the provisions of the Bharatiya Nyaya Sanhita, 2023, and gather relevant evidence, such as work schedules, payment records, and communication logs, to support their claims.

3. Labour Unions: Labour unions can play a crucial role in advocating for the rights of gig workers and challenging misclassification practices. They can leverage the provisions of the Bharatiya Nyaya Sanhita, 2023, to negotiate fair and equitable

employment arrangements for gig workers and represent their interests in legal proceedings related to misclassification disputes. These case studies illustrate the far-reaching implications of the Bharatiya Nyaya Sanhita, 2023, the Bharatiya Sakshya, 2023, and the Bharatiya Nagarik Suraksha Sanhita, 2023, on various aspects of labour and employment law. They highlight the practical challenges and opportunities that employers, employees, and labour unions may face as they navigate the new legal landscape. By embracing best practices, fostering collaboration, and adhering to the principles enshrined in these landmark codes, stakeholders can contribute to the establishment of a fair, efficient, and progressive labour ecosystem in India.

Case Study 10: The Workplace Discrimination Lawsuit Background: At a prominent financial institution, a group of employees with disabilities filed a lawsuit alleging widespread discrimination in hiring, promotion, and reasonable accommodation practices. The employees claimed that the company failed to provide necessary accommodations, denied them equal opportunities for advancement, and fostered a hostile work environment.

Impact of the New Codes: The Bharatiya Nyaya Sanhita, 2023, played a pivotal role in addressing this workplace discrimination case. The code's provisions on non-discrimination, equal opportunity, and reasonable accommodation established clear legal obligations for employers to ensure an inclusive and equitable work environment for individuals with disabilities.

Furthermore, the Bharatiya Sakshya, 2023, facilitated the admissibility and evaluation of various forms of evidence in support of the employees' claims. This included witness testimonies, internal communications, and expert opinions on the company's failure to comply with disability accommodation requirements.

Practical Implications: Employers: Organizations must develop and implement comprehensive policies and procedures to prevent discrimination against individuals with disabilities, in accordance with the provisions of the Bharatiya Nyaya Sanhita, 2023. This includes providing reasonable accommodations, ensuring equal opportunities for hiring and promotion, and fostering an inclusive workplace culture that values diversity and equal treatment.

Employees: The new codes empower individuals with disabilities to assert their rights to non-discrimination, equal opportunity, and reasonable accommodation in the workplace. Employees should familiarize themselves with their organization's policies and the legal protections afforded by the Bharatiya Nyaya Sanhita, 2023. They should maintain detailed records and documentation to support any claims of discrimination or failure to provide reasonable accommodations.

Labour Unions: Labour unions can play a vital role in advocating for the rights of employees with disabilities and ensuring that employers comply with the provisions of the Bharatiya Nyaya Sanhita, 2023. Unions can collaborate with employers to develop inclusive policies, provide guidance and representation to employees facing discrimination, and raise awareness about disability rights and accommodations in the workplace.

Case Study 11: The Unfair Dismissal Claim Background: A long-tenured employee at a manufacturing company was abruptly terminated without proper notice or due process. The employee alleged that the termination was unjustified and violated established procedures for disciplinary actions and dismissals outlined in the company's employee handbook and labor regulations.

Impact of the New Codes: The Bharatiya Nyaya Sanhita, 2023, played a crucial role in addressing this unfair dismissal claim. The code's provisions on employment contracts, termination procedures, and due process established clear guidelines for employers regarding the circumstances and processes for terminating employees.

Additionally, the Bharatiya Sakshya, 2023, facilitated the admissibility and evaluation of various forms of evidence, such as employment records, performance evaluations, and witness accounts, which were crucial in determining whether the termination was justified and followed proper procedures.

Practical Implications: Employers: Organizations must develop and implement clear and transparent policies and procedures for disciplinary actions and terminations, in accordance with the provisions of the Bharatiya Nyaya Sanhita, 2023. These policies should outline the grounds for termination, provide for due process and proper notice periods, and ensure that employees are treated fairly and equitably.

Employees: The new codes empower employees to challenge unfair or unjustified terminations and assert their rights to due process and fair treatment in the workplace. Employees should familiarize themselves with their organization's policies and the legal protections afforded by the Bharatiya Nyaya Sanhita, 2023. They should maintain detailed records and documentation related to their employment history and any disciplinary actions taken against them.

Labour Unions: Labour unions can play a crucial role in advocating for fair and transparent termination procedures and representing employees in unfair dismissal claims. They can negotiate collective bargaining agreements that outline clear guidelines for disciplinary actions and terminations, and provide legal representation to employees who believe they have been unfairly dismissed.

Case Study 12: The Workplace Bullying and Harassment Investigation Background: At a large retail corporation, multiple employees filed complaints alleging a pervasive culture of bullying and harassment by supervisors and managers. The complaints detailed instances of verbal abuse, intimidation, and hostile behavior that created a toxic work environment.

Impact of the New Codes: The Bharatiya Nyaya Sanhita, 2023, played a pivotal role in addressing this workplace bullying and harassment case. The code's provisions on workplace conduct, harassment, and safe working conditions established legal obligations for employers to maintain a respectful and harassment-free work environment.

Furthermore, the Bharatiya Sakshya, 2023, facilitated the admissibility and evaluation of various forms of evidence in support of the employees' claims. This included witness testimonies, contemporaneous documentation of incidents, and expert opinions on the psychological impact of workplace bullying and harassment.

Practical Implications: Employers: Organizations must develop and implement comprehensive anti-bullying and anti-harassment policies and procedures, in accordance with the provisions of the Bharatiya Nyaya Sanhita, 2023. These policies should clearly define unacceptable behavior, establish reporting mechanisms, and outline procedures for investigating and addressing complaints in a timely and effective manner. Employees: The new codes empower employees to report instances of workplace bullying and harassment without fear of retaliation or reprisal. Employees should familiarize themselves with their organization's policies and the legal protections afforded by the Bharatiya Nyaya Sanhita, 2023. They should maintain detailed records and documentation to support their claims and seek assistance from relevant authorities or legal counsel if necessary.

Labour Unions: Labour unions can play a vital role in advocating for safe and respectful work environments free from bullying and harassment. They can collaborate with employers to develop and implement effective anti-bullying and anti-harassment policies, provide support and representation to employees who have experienced such behavior, and ensure that employers adhere to the provisions of the Bharatiya Nyaya Sanhita, 2023.

Case Study 13: The Equal Opportunity in Hiring Dispute Background: A prominent technology company faced allegations of discriminatory hiring practices based on gender and ethnicity. A group of applicants claimed that the company's recruitment processes, including resume screening and interview practices, unfairly disadvantaged certain groups and perpetuated systemic biases.

Impact of the New Codes: The Bharatiya Nyaya Sanhita, 2023, played a crucial role in addressing this equal opportunity in hiring dispute. The code's provisions on non-discrimination, equal opportunity, and fair employment practices established legal obligations for employers to ensure equitable and unbiased recruitment processes.

Additionally, the Bharatiya Sakshya, 2023, facilitated the admissibility and evaluation of various forms of evidence in support of the applicants' claims. This included statistical analyses of hiring data, internal communications, and expert testimonies on the company's recruitment practices and potential biases.

Practical Implications: Employers: Organizations must develop and implement fair and equitable hiring practices that are free from discrimination based on gender, ethnicity, or any other protected characteristics, in accordance with the provisions of the Bharatiya Nyaya Sanhita, 2023. This includes conducting regular audits of recruitment processes, implementing bias-mitigation strategies, and ensuring transparency and objectivity in candidate evaluation and selection.

Applicants: The new codes empower job applicants to challenge discriminatory hiring practices and assert their rights to equal opportunity and fair treatment in the recruitment process. Applicants should familiarize themselves with the legal protections afforded by the Bharatiya Nyaya Sanhita, 2023, and maintain detailed records and documentation related to their job applications and any perceived instances of discrimination.

Labour Unions: Labour unions can play a vital role in advocating for equal opportunity and fair employment practices in hiring. They can collaborate with employers to review and improve recruitment processes, provide guidance and representation to applicants facing discrimination, and ensure that employers adhere to the provisions of the Bharatiya Nyaya Sanhita, 2023.

Case Study 14: The Workplace Safety Whistleblower Retaliation Background: A concerned employee at a manufacturing plant reported numerous safety violations and hazardous working conditions to regulatory authorities. After the authorities launched an investigation based on the employee's report, the company terminated the employee's employment, citing "performance issues" as the reason.

Impact of the New Codes: The Bharatiya Nyaya Sanhita, 2023, played a crucial role in addressing this case of workplace safety whistleblower retaliation. The code's provisions on whistleblower protection and anti-retaliation measures established legal safeguards for employees who report safety concerns or violations in good faith.

Furthermore, the Bharatiya Sakshya, 2023, facilitated the admissibility and evaluation of various forms of evidence in support of the employee's claims. This included the employee's contemporaneous reports, communication records with regulatory authorities, and expert testimonies on the severity of the safety violations.

Practical Implications: Employers: Organizations must develop and implement robust whistleblower protection policies and procedures, in accordance with the provisions of the Bharatiya Nyaya Sanhita, 2023. These policies should encourage employees to report safety concerns or violations without fear of retaliation, establish clear reporting mechanisms, and outline procedures for investigating and addressing such reports in a timely and effective manner.

Employees: The new codes empower employees to report workplace safety concerns or violations without fear of retaliation or adverse employment actions. Employees should familiarize themselves with their organization's whistleblower policies and the legal protections afforded by the Bharatiya Nyaya Sanhita, 2023. They should maintain detailed records and documentation to support their claims and seek assistance from relevant authorities or legal counsel if necessary.

Labour Unions: Labour unions can play a vital role in advocating for workplace safety and whistleblower protection. They can collaborate with employers to develop and implement effective safety and whistleblower policies, provide support and representation to employees who face retaliation for reporting safety concerns, and ensure that employers adhere to the provisions of the Bharatiya Nyaya Sanhita, 2023.

Case Study 15: The Wage Theft and Unpaid Overtime Claim Background: A group of employees at a retail chain filed a collective action lawsuit alleging widespread wage theft and unpaid overtime. The employees claimed that the company routinely failed to compensate them for overtime hours worked, engaged in improper wage deductions, and violated minimum wage laws.

Impact of the New Codes: The Bharatiya Nyaya Sanhita, 2023, played a crucial role in addressing this wage theft and unpaid overtime claim. The code's provisions on minimum wage requirements, overtime compensation, and fair wage practices established legal obligations for employers to properly compensate their employees for all hours worked.

Additionally, the Bharatiya Sakshya, 2023, facilitated the admissibility and evaluation of various forms of evidence in support of the employees' claims. This included time records, payroll data, and expert analyses of the company's wage and hour practices.

Practical Implications: Employers: Organizations must develop and implement accurate time-keeping and payroll systems, in accordance with the provisions of the Bharatiya Nyaya Sanhita, 2023. These systems should ensure that employees are properly compensated for all hours worked, including overtime, and that deductions and wage calculations comply with minimum wage laws and fair wage practices.

Employees: The new codes empower employees to assert their rights to fair compensation and challenge wage theft or unpaid overtime practices. Employees should familiarize themselves with their organization's wage and hour policies, as well as the legal protections afforded by the Bharatiya Nyaya Sanhita, 2023. They should maintain detailed records of their work hours and pay stubs to support any claims of wage violations.

Labour Unions: Labour unions can play a vital role in advocating for fair wage practices and combating wage theft and unpaid overtime. They can negotiate collective bargaining agreements that outline clear wage and hour provisions, provide guidance and representation to employees in wage claims, and ensure that employers adhere to the provisions of the Bharatiya Nyaya Sanhita, 2023.

Case Study 16: The Cross-Border Employment Dispute (Part 2) Background: Following the initial cross-border employment dispute (Case Study 3), GlobalTech Solutions faced another legal challenge from a group of Indian employees working at its subsidiary in Singapore. This time, the employees alleged that the company had failed to provide adequate maternity and parental leave benefits, in violation of Indian labour laws and international conventions.

Impact of the New Codes: The Bharatiya Nyaya Sanhita, 2023, played a crucial role in addressing this cross-border employment dispute related to maternity and parental leave benefits. The code's provisions on employment standards, non-discrimination, and the application of Indian labour laws to employees working for Indian companies or their subsidiaries abroad provided a legal framework for addressing the employees' claims.

Furthermore, the Bharatiya Sakshya, 2023, facilitated the admissibility and evaluation of various forms of evidence in support of the employees' claims. This included employment contracts, company policies, and expert testimonies on the applicable international conventions and best practices regarding maternity and parental leave.

Practical Implications: Employers: Multinational companies and those with cross-border operations must ensure compliance with the labour laws and regulations of the countries in which they operate, as well as the provisions of the Bharatiya Nyaya Sanhita, 2023, regarding the rights and protections afforded to employees of Indian companies or their subsidiaries abroad. Employers should review their maternity and parental leave policies and practices to align with Indian labour laws and international standards.

Employees: The new codes empower employees working for Indian companies or their subsidiaries abroad to assert their rights to maternity and parental leave benefits, in accordance with Indian labour laws and international conventions. Employees should familiarize themselves with the legal protections afforded by the Bharatiya Nyaya Sanhita, 2023, and maintain records and documentation related to their employment contracts and any instances of maternity or parental leave being denied or restricted.

Labour Unions: Labour unions can play a crucial role in advocating for the rights of Indian workers employed by multinational companies or their subsidiaries abroad. They can collaborate with international counterparts and leverage the provisions of the Bharatiya Nyaya Sanhita,

2023, to ensure that employers provide adequate maternity and parental leave benefits, in compliance with Indian labour laws and international standards.

These additional case studies further illustrate the wide-ranging implications of the Bharatiya Nyaya Sanhita, 2023, the Bharatiya Sakshya, 2023, and the Bharatiya Nagarik Suraksha Sanhita, 2023, in various areas of labour and employment law. They highlight the practical challenges and opportunities that employers, employees, and labour unions may face as they navigate issues such as workplace discrimination, unfair dismissal, bullying and harassment, equal opportunity in hiring, whistleblower retaliation, wage theft, and cross-border employment disputes. By understanding and adhering to the principles and provisions of these comprehensive codes, stakeholders can contribute to the establishment of a fair, inclusive, and progressive labour ecosystem in India

7.2 Conclusion

Navigating the complexities of the Bharatiya Nyaya Sanhita, 2023, the Bharatiya Sakshya, 2023, and the Bharatiya Nagarik Suraksha Sanhita, 2023, requires a proactive and comprehensive approach to compliance and dispute resolution. Employers, employees, and labour unions must adopt best practices to ensure a smooth transition to the new legal regime and foster a fair, efficient, and progressive labour and employment ecosystem in India.

1. Conduct Comprehensive Legal Audits Employers should undertake thorough legal audits to assess their compliance with the provisions of the new codes. This involves a systematic review and evaluation of various aspects of their operations,

practices, and policies to identify potential areas of non-compliance.

1.1. Review of Employment Contracts and Policies Employers should critically examine their existing employment contracts, employee handbooks, and related policies to ensure alignment with the new legal requirements. This includes reviewing provisions related to hiring, compensation, benefits, leave entitlements, workplace safety, non-discrimination, and dispute resolution mechanisms.

1.2. Assessment of Labour Practices Employers should assess their labour practices, such as recruitment processes, performance evaluation methods, disciplinary procedures, and termination protocols. These practices must be scrutinized for compliance with the principles of non-discrimination, equal opportunity, due process, and fair treatment as enshrined in the Bharatiya Nyaya Sanhita, 2023.

1.3. Evaluation of Workplace Safety and Health Measures The legal audit should also encompass an evaluation of workplace safety and health measures. This includes assessing compliance with the provisions of the Bharatiya Nagarik Suraksha Sanhita, 2023, regarding risk assessments, emergency preparedness, personal protective equipment, and occupational health and safety protocols.

1.4. Identification of Potential Areas of Non-Compliance Through a comprehensive legal audit, employers can identify potential areas of non-compliance and take proactive steps to address them. Engaging legal professionals and subject matter experts can provide valuable insights and guidance during this process.

By conducting thorough legal audits, employers can mitigate legal risks, avoid potential liabilities, and ensure a smooth transition to the new legal regime.

    2. Develop Robust Internal Compliance Programs Employers should establish robust internal compliance programs that encompass training, monitoring, and reporting mechanisms to ensure adherence to the new codes.

2.1. Comprehensive Training and Awareness Initiatives Employers should develop and implement comprehensive training programs to educate employees at all levels about the new codes, their rights and responsibilities, and the organization's policies and procedures related to compliance. These training initiatives should be tailored to different roles and responsibilities within the organization and should be conducted regularly to reinforce the importance of compliance.

2.2. Effective Monitoring and Reporting Mechanisms Effective monitoring and reporting mechanisms are crucial for identifying and addressing potential violations or areas of concern promptly. This may involve establishing dedicated compliance teams, implementing whistleblower hotlines, and encouraging employees to report any concerns or irregularities without fear of retaliation.

2.3. Periodic Compliance Audits and Reviews Employers should conduct periodic compliance audits and reviews to assess the effectiveness of their internal compliance programs. These audits should evaluate the implementation and adherence to established policies and procedures, identify areas for improvement, and recommend corrective actions where necessary.

2.4. Collaboration with Legal and Compliance Experts Employers should consider collaborating with legal professionals and compliance experts to ensure that their internal compliance programs are up-to-date and aligned with the latest legal developments and best practices. These experts can provide valuable guidance on interpreting and implementing the new codes and assist in developing robust compliance strategies.

By developing robust internal compliance programs, employers can foster a culture of accountability, transparency, and ethical conduct within their organizations, reducing the risk of non-compliance and potential legal liabilities.

3. Embrace Alternative Dispute Resolution (ADR) Mechanisms The new codes encourage the use of alternative dispute resolution (ADR) mechanisms, such as mediation and arbitration, for resolving labour and employment disputes. Employers and employees should explore these cost-effective and time-efficient options as an alternative to traditional litigation.

3.1. Mediation Mediation is a voluntary and non-binding process in which a neutral third party (mediator) facilitates communication and negotiation between the parties involved in a dispute. The mediator assists the parties in identifying their interests, exploring options, and reaching a mutually acceptable resolution.

3.2. Arbitration Arbitration is a private and binding dispute resolution process in which the parties agree to have their dispute resolved by an impartial third party (arbitrator) or a panel of arbitrators. The arbitrator's decision is legally binding and enforceable, providing a final resolution to the dispute.

3.3. Advantages of ADR Mechanisms ADR mechanisms offer several advantages over traditional litigation, including:

- Cost-effectiveness: ADR processes are typically less expensive than lengthy and complex court proceedings.
- Time efficiency: ADR processes are generally faster than traditional litigation, allowing for a more expeditious resolution of disputes.
- Confidentiality: ADR proceedings are typically confidential, protecting the privacy of the parties involved and avoiding potential reputational damage.
- Preservation of relationships: ADR mechanisms foster a more collaborative and amicable resolution process, which can help preserve valuable business relationships and minimize disruptions.

3.4. Integration of ADR into Dispute Resolution Policies Employers should consider integrating ADR mechanisms into their dispute resolution policies and employment contracts. This may involve establishing clear procedures for initiating ADR processes, selecting mediators or arbitrators, and enforcing any resulting agreements or decisions.

By embracing ADR mechanisms, employers and employees can benefit from a more efficient and cost-effective approach to resolving labour and employment disputes, while fostering a collaborative and constructive environment for conflict resolution.

4. Strengthen Grievance Redressal Processes Employers should review and strengthen their internal grievance redressal processes to ensure they align with the provisions of the new codes.

Effective grievance redressal mechanisms can help address employee concerns and disputes promptly, before they escalate into legal proceedings.

4.1. Clear and Accessible Grievance Procedures Employers should establish clear and well-defined procedures for employees to raise grievances or concerns related to their employment, working conditions, or workplace issues. These procedures should be easily accessible and communicated to all employees, ensuring transparency and fairness.

4.2. Impartial and Timely Grievance Resolution The grievance redressal process should involve impartial and timely resolution mechanisms. This may include designated grievance committees or ombudspersons responsible for investigating and addressing complaints in an unbiased and expeditious manner.

4.3. Confidentiality and Non-Retaliation Protections Employees should be assured of confidentiality and non-retaliation protections when raising grievances or concerns. Employers should implement robust policies and procedures to safeguard employees from any form of retaliation or adverse consequences for raising legitimate grievances in good faith.

4.4. Continuous Improvement and Feedback Mechanisms Employers should regularly review and seek feedback on their grievance redressal processes to identify areas for improvement. This may involve conducting employee surveys, analyzing trends in grievances, and implementing necessary changes to enhance the effectiveness and efficiency of the processes.

By strengthening their grievance redressal processes, employers can foster a positive workplace culture, promote open communication, and address potential issues before they escalate into formal disputes or legal proceedings.

5. Foster Collaboration and Social Dialogue Labour unions and employers should prioritize collaboration and social dialogue in navigating the new legal landscape. Regular consultations, open communication channels, and a willingness to engage in constructive negotiations can help address potential areas of conflict, promote mutual understanding, and facilitate the development of sustainable solutions that benefit all stakeholders.

5.1. Establishment of Joint Consultative Committees Employers and labour unions should consider establishing joint consultative committees or forums to facilitate regular dialogue and consultations on matters related to the implementation of the new codes, workplace policies, and labour-management relations.

5.2. Collective Bargaining and Negotiation Collective bargaining and negotiation processes should be conducted in good faith, with a focus on finding mutually beneficial solutions. This may involve negotiating collective agreements that incorporate the provisions of the new codes and address issues such as wages, benefits, working conditions, and dispute resolution mechanisms.

5.3. Capacity Building and Training Employers and labour unions should invest in capacity-building initiatives and training programs to enhance their understanding of the new legal framework and develop effective strategies for collaboration and social dialogue. This may involve engaging subject matter experts, legal professionals, and industry associations to provide guidance and training.

5.4. Dispute Resolution and Grievance Handling In the event of disputes or grievances, employers and labour unions should prioritize open communication, good-faith negotiations, and the utilization of alternative dispute resolution mechanisms, such as mediation and arbitration, before resorting to legal proceedings.

By fostering collaboration and social dialogue, employers and labour unions can build trust, promote industrial harmony, and jointly navigate the complexities of the new legal landscape, fostering a progressive and sustainable labour and employment ecosystem.

6. Stay Updated on Legal Developments The Bharatiya Nyaya Sanhita, 2023, the Bharatiya Sakshya, 2023, and the Bharatiya Nagarik Suraksha Sanhita, 2023, represent a dynamic and evolving legal framework. It is crucial for employers, employees, and labour unions to stay updated on any amendments, judicial interpretations, or regulatory changes that may impact the application and implementation of the codes.

6.1. Monitoring Legislative and Regulatory Updates Employers, employees, and labour unions should actively monitor legislative and regulatory updates related to the new codes. This may involve subscribing to relevant publications, attending seminars or webinars, and engaging with industry associations or legal experts to stay informed about the latest developments.

6.2. Tracking Judicial Interpretations Judicial interpretations of the new codes by courts and tribunals can have significant implications for their application and implementation. Employers, employees, and labour unions should closely follow relevant court cases and judicial decisions to understand how the provisions of the codes are being interpreted and applied in practice.

6.3. Participation in Industry Forums and Knowledge-Sharing Platforms Participating in industry forums, conferences, and knowledge-sharing platforms can provide valuable insights and opportunities to engage with peers, legal professionals, and subject matter experts. These platforms can facilitate the exchange of best practices, lessons learned, and strategies for navigating the new legal landscape.

6.4. Engagement with Legal Professionals and Consultants Engaging legal professionals and consultants can be beneficial for employers, employees, and labour unions seeking expert guidance on interpreting and complying with the new codes. These professionals can provide tailored advice, conduct legal audits, and assist in developing compliance strategies aligned with the latest legal developments.

By staying updated on legal developments, stakeholders can proactively adapt their practices, policies, and strategies, ensuring continuous compliance with the evolving legal framework and mitigating potential risks and liabilities.

7. Leverage Technology and Data Analytics In today's digital age, employers can leverage technology and data analytics to enhance their compliance efforts and streamline dispute resolution processes. Implementing digital record-keeping systems, automated compliance monitoring tools, and data-driven analytics can help identify potential risks, track performance, and inform decision-making processes related to labour and employment matters.

7.1. Digital Record-Keeping Systems Employers should consider implementing digital record-keeping systems to maintain accurate and comprehensive records related to employment contracts, policies, attendance, payroll, and other relevant data. These systems can facilitate efficient data management, ensure data integrity, and enable easy access and retrieval of information when required.

7.2. Automated Compliance Monitoring Tools Automated compliance monitoring tools can assist employers in tracking and monitoring compliance with various aspects of the new codes, such as wage and hour regulations, leave entitlements, and workplace safety requirements. These tools can provide real-time alerts and notifications, enabling employers to take timely corrective actions and mitigate potential risks.

7.3. Data-Driven Analytics By collecting and analyzing data related to employment practices, workplace incidents, grievances, and disputes, employers can gain valuable insights and identify patterns or trends that may require attention or intervention. Data-driven analytics can inform decision-making processes, enabling employers to implement targeted strategies and preventive measures to address potential issues proactively.

7.4. Integration of Technology and Compliance Programs Employers should integrate technology and data analytics into their overall compliance programs, ensuring that these tools and systems are aligned with the organization's policies, procedures, and legal obligations under the new codes. Regular training and support should be provided to employees to effectively utilize these technologies and leverage their full potential.

By leveraging technology and data analytics, employers can streamline their compliance efforts, enhance transparency, and make informed decisions, ultimately fostering a more efficient and effective labour and employment ecosystem.

8. Promote Ethical Business Practices Compliance with the Bharatiya Nyaya Sanhita, 2023, the Bharatiya Sakshya, 2023, and the Bharatiya Nagarik Suraksha Sanhita, 2023, should be viewed not merely as a legal obligation, but as an opportunity to promote ethical business practices and foster a culture of integrity within organizations. Employers should emphasize the importance of ethical conduct, transparency, and corporate social responsibility, aligning their values and practices with the principles enshrined in the new legal framework.

8.1. Development of Ethical Codes of Conduct Employers should develop and implement comprehensive codes of conduct that reflect the organization's commitment to ethical business practices, social responsibility, and adherence to legal and regulatory requirements. These codes should serve as guiding principles for all employees, fostering a culture of integrity and accountability.

8.2. Integration of Ethics and Compliance Training Ethics and compliance training should be an integral part of an organization's training programs. Employees at all levels should receive regular training on ethical decision-making, recognizing and addressing ethical dilemmas, and understanding the organization's commitment to ethical conduct and compliance with the new codes.

8.3. Establishment of Ethical Governance Structures Employers should consider establishing ethical governance structures, such as ethics committees or advisory boards, to provide guidance on ethical issues, monitor compliance with ethical standards, and promote a culture of integrity within the organization.

8.4. Whistleblower Protection and Reporting Mechanisms Employers should implement robust whistleblower protection policies and reporting mechanisms to encourage employees to report unethical or illegal conduct without fear of retaliation. These mechanisms should be accessible, confidential, and supported by a clear investigation and resolution process.

8.5. Corporate Social Responsibility Initiatives Employers should actively engage in corporate social responsibility (CSR) initiatives that align with the principles of the new codes and demonstrate their commitment to sustainable and responsible business practices. These initiatives may include community outreach programs, environmental sustainability efforts, and initiatives aimed at promoting workplace diversity and inclusion.

By promoting ethical business practices, employers can not only ensure compliance with the new legal framework but also foster a positive organizational culture, enhance their reputation, and contribute to the broader societal goals of promoting fairness, transparency, and responsible business conduct.

In conclusion, navigating the complexities of the Bharatiya Nyaya Sanhita, 2023, the Bharatiya Sakshya, 2023, and the Bharatiya Nagarik Suraksha Sanhita, 2023, requires a proactive and comprehensive approach to compliance and dispute resolution. By embracing best practices such as conducting comprehensive legal audits, developing robust internal compliance programs, embracing alternative dispute resolution mechanisms, strengthening grievance redressal processes, fostering collaboration and social dialogue, staying updated on legal developments, leveraging technology and data analytics, and promoting ethical business practices, employers, employees, and labour unions can contribute to the establishment of a fair, efficient, and progressive labour and employment ecosystem.

VISHAL YADAV

Vishal Yadav is an alumnus of Maharshi Dayanand University (MDU) in Rohtak. MDU is known for its robust academic programs and emphasis on research and development across various disciplines. Vishal pursued his Bachelor of Laws (LL.B.) from the University of Rajasthan, located in Jaipur. This institution is renowned for its comprehensive law programs, providing a strong foundation in legal principles, practices, and ethics. In addition to his law degree, Vishal holds a Postgraduate Diploma in Criminology. This advanced study has equipped him with specialized knowledge in the field of criminology, including the analysis of criminal behavior, criminal justice systems, and crime prevention strategies.

Vishal Yadav combines his legal expertise with a specialized understanding of criminology, making him a valuable asset in the legal and criminological fields. His educational journey reflects a commitment to understanding the law and its application to societal issues, particularly in the realm of crime and justice.

Observations and Scientific Contributions

Natural Selection: People who possess favorable qualities have a higher chance of surviving, procreating, and transferring those traits to the next generation.

Descent with Modification: Over extended periods, natural selection accumulates modifications that give rise to the emergence of new species.

Acknowledgment and Effect: Upon its release, "On the Origin of Species" provoked discussion and controversy right away. It presented a naturalistic explanation for the variety of life and refuted the widely held belief that species are permanent and unchanging. Many scientists, including well-known biologists, backed the hypothesis, despite the opposition of certain scientists and religious leaders. As more and more evidence for evolution was gathered throughout time, his hypothesis gained traction.

Additional Research and Upcoming Projects

Introduction to the Theory: Darwin's theories were refined and extended in later publications. The idea of evolution was applied to the origins of humans in "The Descent of Man, and Selection about Sex" (1871), which proposed a common ancestor between humans and apes. Additionally, he established the idea of sexual selection, which favors characteristics that increase an individual's likelihood of mating.

Studies of Botany: In his later writings, he conducted in-depth research on plants. He examined how plants adapted to their surroundings in "The Power of Movement in Plants" (1880) and other botanical writings, which provided more evidence for his theories on natural selection.

Well-being and Heritage: Up until his death on April 19, 1882, he worked and published despite persistent health problems. Beyond his writings, he had a significant impact on a wide range of scientific disciplines, including biology, geology, and anthropology. His grave at Westminster Abbey is a testament to his great influence on both science and society.

In Conclusion, his early hobbies, schooling, mentoring, and extensive research on the HMS Beagle voyage all had an impact on his difficult process of developing the idea of evolution by natural selection. His capacity to integrate many thoughts and facts into a logical system fundamentally altered our perception of Earthly existence. Darwin's work is still a pillar of science since it established the framework for contemporary evolutionary biology. One of the most significant and enduring scientific hypotheses ever put out, evolution by natural selection has had a tremendous impact on how we see the natural world.

Chapter 2

Regarding the Species' Origin

19th-century Scientific Environment: An important era of scientific research and discovery occurred in the middle of the 19th century. Numerous species have been classified and cataloged as a result of naturalists' massive global data collection efforts. The consensus, on the other hand, was that species were fixed, having evolved independently and without change from the beginning of time. This position was supported by the prevailing scientific and theological viewpoint, which was inspired by Carl Linnaeus and Georges Cuvier.

Several scientists had started to doubt the static notion of species before him. An early hypothesis of evolution put out by Jean-Baptiste Lamarck postulated that qualities acquired by organisms might be passed on during their lifetimes.

Lamarck's theory of heredity was eventually shown to be false, but he was affected by his theories on species evolution. Additionally, his ideas of long-term, progressive biological changes were greatly inspired by Charles Lyell's "Principles of Geology," which promoted uniformitarianism, or steady geological processes.

HMS Beagle's Voyage: The HMS Beagle's five-year journey from 1831 to 1836 had a significant influence on his theories. It was his observations of different species in different habitats, especially in South America and the Galápagos Islands, that made him wonder whether one species might change into another species. He observed differences across species that seemed to be tailored to their particular settings, suggesting a process of evolution.

Theoretical Formulation: Following his return from the expedition, he spent twenty years collecting data and honing his theories about evolution. He developed the theory of natural selection as a result of reading Thomas Malthus's article on population expansion, which emphasized the struggle for resources. He came to understand that people who had desirable qualities had a higher chance of surviving, procreating, and transferring those traits to the next generation. The slow accumulation of these modifications may result in the emergence of new species.

Release and Primary Response: At first, he was hesitant to share his theories because he knew they may cause controversy. Nonetheless, Alfred Russel Wallace independently developed a theory of natural selection that was comparable to him in 1858. He decided to publish his research as a result. On November 24, 1859, the book "On the Origin of Species Using Natural Selection" was released. The first 1,250 copies of the book were sold out right away, indicating strong interest and discussion.

Organisation and Content

Preface: He gives a short overview of the book's goals and the background to the species controversy in the introduction. He lays forth the foundation for his argument and appreciates the contributions of earlier naturalists.

First Chapter: Diversity in Domestication: He starts by talking about the variations seen in domesticated plants and animals, such as pigeons, dogs, and crops. He contends that if artificial selection, or selective breeding, can lead to major changes in humankind, then natural selection may have a comparable effect on wild animals.

Part 11: Diversity In Nature: The subject of natural diversity among species is further upon in this chapter. He highlights that variety is a normal occurrence and that it is necessary for natural selection to work. He uses a plethora of instances from his observations to highlight the variation in features across different animals.

Chapter 111: The Battle for Survival: He presents the notion of the "struggle for existence," drawing on the population increase theories of Malthus. He argues that when an organism produces more children than it can support, competition for few resources results. Natural selection is driven in part by this battle.

Natural Selection in Chapter 1V: Darwin provides an overview of the principles of natural selection in this important chapter. He describes how people who possess advantageous variants have a higher chance of surviving, procreating, and transferring those qualities to the next generation. This mechanism eventually results in species adaptability and evolution. He also addresses the function of sexual selection, which favors characteristics that increase the likelihood of a mating success.

Laws of Variation: Chapter V: While conceding that the underlying processes were not completely known in his day, he investigates the origins of variation. He talks about things like how the environment affects things and how organs are used and not used. Even though some of his theories were theoretical, they served as a foundation for later genetic study.

Part VI: Challenges in Theory: The hypothesis resolves several possible problems and criticisms, including the complexity of certain organs and the lack of transitional forms in the fossil record. He shows that he has carefully considered any potential complaints by offering justifications and arguments in response to these challenges.

Instinct in Chapter VII: The function of instinct in animal behavior is examined in this chapter. He contends that natural selection may drive the evolution of instincts just as it does physical features. He demonstrates his thesis with instances of intricate behaviors, such as the construction of bird nests and bee hives.

Hybridism in Chapter VIII: He talks about the sterility of hybrids or children of various species, and how it affects the borders between species. He contends that natural selection keeps species separate, which leads to hybrid sterility.

On the Imperfection of the Geological Record: Chapter IX: He admits that his hypothesis was seriously challenged by the incompleteness of the fossil record. He contends that several issues, including erosion and the scarcity of fossilization, contribute to the imperfection of the geological record. Despite this, he argues that the data at hand favors progressive change over time.

Chapter X: Regarding the Geological Lineage of Living Things: He examines the succession patterns seen in the fossil record in this chapter. He contends that the theory of slow evolution is supported by the orderly emergence and extinction of species. He also talks about the idea of extinction and how biodiversity is shaped by it.

Geographic Distribution: Chapter XI: He looks at how various geographical areas have diverse species distributions. He contends that the distributional patterns provide credence to the theories of common ancestry and the impact of geographic barriers on the development of species. This thesis revolves around his findings of island biogeography, especially in the Galápagos.

Spatial Distribution (continued) in Chapter XII:

He explores the methods of species dispersion, including migration and colonization, to continue the conversation on geographical distribution. He backs up his claims with evidence from several different islands and locations.

Relative Similarities of Living Things: Anatomy, Development, and Basic Organs: He investigates the parallels and discrepancies between species, concentrating on embryology, comparative anatomy, and primitive organs. He contends that these parallels demonstrate the branching pattern of evolution and shared ancestry. Vestigial structures, which are primitive organs, provide evidence in favor of the theory that species evolve throughout time.

Recapitulation and Conclusion in Chapter XIV: He restates his claims and emphasizes the significance of natural selection as the main process underlying evolution in the concluding chapter. He highlights the magnificence of seeing life as the outcome of evolutionary processes and considers the wider implications of his theory for comprehending the natural world.

Significance and Heritage

Prompt Response: After it was published, "On the Origin of Species" attracted a lot of attention and discussion. The theory refuted the prevalent beliefs about fixed species and offered a naturalistic account of life's variety. He theories were rejected by some scientists and religious leaders, but they were embraced by others, including well-known biologists like Thomas Huxley. As additional information was gathered, the early debate eventually gave way to broad acceptance.

Technological Developments: Natural selection, as proposed by him, changed biology and had an impact on many other scientific disciplines. It offered a cohesive framework for comprehending both the mechanisms of species change and life's variety. His theory was further reinforced by subsequent genetic discoveries, especially the work of Gregor Mendel and the creation of the modern synthesis in the 20th century, which supplied the genetic processes behind natural selection.

Further Repercussions: His theories have a significant impact on philosophy, religion, and society in addition to science. Conventional theories of creation and human existence in the natural world were called into question by the notion of evolution. It inspired discussions on ethics, morality, and human behavior as well as reevaluations of humanity's place in nature.

Persistent Impact: Still regarded as one of the most important scientific publications ever, "On the Origin of Species" It has an influence on disciplines like anthropology, psychology, and environmental science in addition to biology. Darwin's theories still influence science today and how we see the natural world.

In Conclusion, the seminal essay "On the Origin of Species" by Charles Darwin drastically altered our perception of life as it exists on Earth. He provided a theory of evolution by natural selection that has lasted the test of time via painstaking observation, careful research, and persuasive explanation. With its release, the book ushered in a new age in science, revolutionizing biology and impacting many other fields. As we continue to investigate and comprehend the intricacies of the natural world, Darwin's legacy lives on.

Additional Study and Publications

Following the release of "On the Origin of Species" in 1859, Charles Darwin carried out more studies and wrote significant books that developed and broadened his views of evolution. His latter writings contributed to the scientific community's comprehension of natural selection and evolution on a variety of subjects, including plant biology and human evolution.

The Origin of Man and Sex-Related Selection (1871), Themes and Content

1. Human Evolution: He extended his theory of evolution to humans in "The Descent of Man," contending that humans and apes had a common origin. He looked at anatomical and psychological characteristics, such as the makeup of the brain, muscles, and bones, to show how humans and other animals are similar. He also discussed the intellectual and moral faculties, putting forward the theory that social behaviors and natural selection led to the evolution of these qualities.

2. *Sexual Selection:* As a process distinct from natural selection, Darwin presented the idea of sexual selection. He clarified that the competition between members of the same sex—typically males—for mates is what leads to sexual selection. Even if these features are not beneficial for survival, this may lead to the development of characteristics that increase mating success, such as complex feathers in birds or antlers in deer.

3. *Impact and Debate:* The implications of "The Descent of Man" for human origins and its refutation of conventional notions of human exceptionalism made it contentious. Discussions on race, gender, and the function of sexual selection in evolution were spurred by the book. His work established the groundwork for contemporary psychology and anthropology, notwithstanding the debate.

The Way Emotions Are Expressed in Humans and Animals, 1872

Themes and Content: In "The Expression of the Emotions," Darwin examined how humans and other species' emotional displays originated in evolution. Numerous utterances, he said, are universal and significant in terms of development. Through his in-depth studies of both people and animals, he study yielded numerous important insights, including:

1. Serviceable Associated Habits: Darwin postulated that the initial meanings of terms were utilitarian. For instance, biting motions may have led to the evolution of baring teeth.

2. Antithesis: Differing mental processes produce opposed utterances. A dog's submissive posture contrasts with its aggressive attitude, for instance.

3. Direct Action of the Neurological System: Regardless of will or habit, the neurological system may directly cause some expressions.

Effect and Heritage: The disciplines of ethology, psychology, and even the study of nonverbal communication were impacted by this work. He bolstered the notion of a common evolutionary past by emphasizing the continuity of animal and human behavior.

Compositae Without Roots (1875)

Themes and Content: His "Insectivorous Plants" explored how certain plants catch and metabolize insects. He carried out a great deal of research on a variety of carnivorous plants, including pitcher plants, sundews, and the Venus flytrap. He illustrated how these plants evolved specialized structures and behaviors to harvest nutrition from insects to adapt to nutrient-poor situations.

Main Results

1. Mechanisms of Capture: He described the chemical and physical processes that these plants use to ensnare and break down their food. He explained, for instance, how sensitive hairs on the leaf surface cause the Venus flytrap to close quickly.

2. Digestive Processes: He demonstrated how these plants receive the nutrients that are produced after their prey is digested by identifying the enzymes involved.

Effect and Heritage: The study of insectivorous plants by Darwin advanced our knowledge of plant physiology and adaptability. It emphasized how intricate and creative evolutionary responses to environmental problems can be.

The Vegetable Kingdom's Repercussions from Cross and Self Fertilisation (1876)

Themes and Content: He examined the effects of self-fertilization (inside the same plant) and cross-fertilization (between separate plants) on plant vigor and reproductive success in this book. To compare the effects of these various fertilization techniques, he carried out in-depth research on a wide range of plant species.

Main Results

1. Benefits of Cross-Fertilization: He discovered that, in comparison to self-fertilized plants, cross-fertilized plants tended to be more robust, generating more seeds and healthier progeny.

2. Inbreeding Depression: Reproductive vigor and fertility declined in subsequent generations due to inbreeding depression, which was often caused by self-fertilization.

Effect and Heritage: The significance of outcrossing and genetic variety in preserving healthy populations was emphasized by this study. It also sheds light on the benefits of cross-pollination for evolution and plant breeding techniques.

The Variations in Flower Forms on the Same Species of Plants (1877)

Themes and Content: He investigated the phenomena of heterostyly in this book, which occurs when plants belonging to the same species produce distinct flower types with diverse configurations of reproductive organs. He researched how flower shapes, like primroses, aid in cross-pollination.

Main Results

1. Mechanisms of Heterostyly: He explained how various flower shapes, such as long- and short-styled flowers, ensure that pollen is transmitted between flower types that are compatible and promote cross-pollination.

2. Reproductive Advantages: He showed that more genetic variety and better reproductive success are advantageous to heterostylous plants.

Effect and Heritage: The knowledge of plant reproductive strategies and their evolutionary importance was expanded by his work on heterostyly. It also highlighted how closely plant morphology and pollination processes relate to one another.

The Plants' Ability to Move (1880)

Themes and Content: This book looked at the several kinds of movement that plants exhibit, such as phototropism—the development of shoots towards light—and gravitropism—the movement of roots towards gravity. He carried out several experiments with his son Francis to investigate these motions and the underlying causes.

Main Results

1. **Tropisms:** He recognized the function of environmental cues like gravity and light in guiding plant development.

2. **Circumnutation:** He explained how developing plant components travel in a spiral motion to investigate their surroundings and identify the best growing circumstances.

3. **Auxin:** Although Darwin did not name the particular hormone, his discoveries paved the way for the identification of auxin, a plant hormone that controls growth and motility.

Effect and Heritage: The book "The Power of Movement in Plants" advanced our knowledge of the physiology and behavior of plants. It proved that even though they are sessile, plants are dynamic beings with sophisticated environmental reactions.

The Action of Worms in the Formation of Vegetable Mold (1881)

Themes and Content: The subject of his last work was earthworms' function in the development of soil and ecological processes. Over many decades, he carried out in-depth observations and tests to get an understanding of the role earthworms play in the breakdown of organic materials and the creation of healthy soil.

Main Results

1. Soil Formation: He showed that earthworms are essential for the decomposition of organic matter and the blending of it with mineral soil to produce rich topsoil.

2. *Ecosystem Services:* He emphasized the role that earthworms play in sustaining ecosystems, encouraging plant development, and preserving the health of the soil.

Effect and Heritage: The importance of earthworms in agriculture and ecology was highlighted by this investigation. It also demonstrated his enduring interest in natural phenomena and his dedication to understanding how all life is interrelated.

In Conclusion, He made significant contributions to science much beyond "On the Origin of Species." His later studies and writings covered a wide variety of subjects, each advancing our knowledge of evolution, adaptation, and natural processes. From plant biology and soil creation to human evolution and emotional expression, his work established the groundwork for many scientific fields and still has an impact on current studies. He is now considered to be among the most significant scientists in history due to his thorough observations, rigorous experiments, and perceptive hypotheses, all of which have left a lasting legacy.

Individual Life and Well-being of Darwin's

Family Life and Marriage

Emma Wedgwood's marriage: He tied the knot with Emma Wedgwood, his cousin, on January 29, 1839. Despite having different religious beliefs, the two had a strong friendship and mutual respect. Emma was a devoted Unitarian, whereas he gradually became more and more agnostic. Their union was characterized by love, cooperation in thought, and support for one another. Emma gave him tremendous emotional and practical assistance throughout his life and scientific pursuits.

Three of the 10 children that him and Emma had passed away at a young age. The kids that made it out alive were:

1. Banker William Erasmus Darwin (1839–1914)

2. Early in life, Anne Elizabeth Darwin (1841–1851) passed away.

3. Shortly after her birth, Mary Eleanor Darwin (1842–1842) passed away.

4. Many of Darwin's writings were edited by Henrietta Emma Darwin (1843–1929).

5. Mathematician and astronomer George Howard Darwin (1845–1912)

6. Elizabeth Darwin (1847–1926) was a reclusive person.

7. Editor of Darwin's publications and a botanist, Francis Darwin (1848–1925)

8. Born in 1850, Leonard Darwin was a politician, eugenicist, and soldier.

9. Engineer Horace Darwin, who founded the Cambridge Scientific Instrument Company, lived from 1851 to 1828.

10. The infant Charles Waring Darwin (1856–1858) died.

As a loving father, he placed a high value on the development and well-being of his kids. He turned his house into an unofficial laboratory by including them in many of his observations and experiments.

Health Concerns

He spent most of his adult life dealing with a variety of chronic health conditions. In addition to significant gastrointestinal issues, he also had headaches, heart palpitations, exhaustion, and skin rashes. He was often rendered disabled by these symptoms, which made him withdraw to Down House, his house in Kent, where he could control his illness in a somewhat comfortable manner.

His ailment was never conclusively identified during his lifetime, despite several consultations with doctors. Regarding the nature of his ailment, contemporary medical historians and physicians have conjectured and offered several diagnoses, such as:

Chagas Disease: He may have acquired this persistent parasite illness when visiting South America. Although there isn't enough proof to draw firm conclusions, the symptoms match many of his concerns.

Irritable Bowel Syndrome (IBS) or Crohn's Disease: These illnesses may be the cause of his severe gastrointestinal problems.

Psychosomatic Illness: Given the contentious nature of his work and his disputes over religion, some speculate that his symptoms may have been made worse by stress and worry.

Affect on Work: His health problems had a big influence on his work habits and day-to-day activities. To regulate his symptoms, he devised a rigorous routine that comprised rest times, little activity, and a restricted diet. He was nevertheless extraordinarily industrious despite his ailments. He produced a significant corpus of scientific work because he could work regularly, even in short spurts.

Daily Schedule and Way of Life

A resident of Down House: Down House became his primary home for the remainder of his life when he and his family relocated there in 1842. The tranquility of the rural surroundings suited his demands for both work and wellness. He could also carry out many of his experiments at Down House, especially those about plant biology.

Regular Schedule: His daily schedule was set up to maximize his output despite his health issues.

Morning: He usually worked for around an hour and a half before breakfast, starting his day early.

Late Morning: He worked till late in the morning after breakfast, often concentrating on writing and communications.

Afternoon: he would work on simpler scientific projects, such as reviewing experimental findings or reading scientific literature, after a midday stroll, lunch, and a brief nap.

Evening: He enjoyed reading and playing backgammon with his family throughout the evening. Sometimes, if he felt good enough, he would work into the evening.

Recreation & Leisure: He took pleasure in a wide range of pastimes. He loved reading, especially poetry and novels. Long walks and other outdoor activities were enjoyable pursuits for him as well, since they served as a source of physical activity and creative inspiration. In addition to being places of relaxation, his garden and greenhouse at Down House were the locations of many of his botanical experiments.

Social Life and Relationships

He kept up tight ties with his family and a group of acquaintances, many of whom were scholars and scientists. His scientific and personal communication with other scientists, including Asa Grey, Thomas Huxley, and Joseph Dalton Hooker, was fruitful. These connections were essential to the development and dissemination of his theories.

He was a rather quiet man, despite his enormous influence on society. He hardly ever attended meetings or took part in public scientific disputes. This was caused in part by his health issues as well as his desire for a peaceful life devoted to study. He was happy to allow others, such as Huxley, to publicly support and argue his beliefs. His opinions on religion changed over his life. Coming from a religious family, his first career goal was to become a preacher. He began to doubt conventional religious ideas, nonetheless, as a result of his scientific findings. By the time he wrote "On the Origin of Species," he had declared himself an agnostic, seeing religion and science as two distinct domains.

Subsequent Times and Legacy

Ongoing Projects and Publications: Up until his death, he worked on several scientific endeavors despite his persistent health problems. He published important studies on botany, geology, and animal behavior later in life. Every publication advanced the knowledge and acceptance of evolutionary theory.

Death: On April 19, 1882, he passed away at Down House. Heart disease was the official cause of death, but there's no denying that his long-term medical conditions had some influence. He received the distinction of being buried in Westminster Abbey, which recognized his important contributions to science.

Historical: His contributions to science go far beyond his seminal work on evolution. He is known for being an industrious researcher, a loving husband and father, and a philosopher whose theories revolutionized how we see the natural world. His contributions served as a springboard for contemporary biology and still have an impact on science today. His modesty, tenacity in the face of a debilitating sickness, and commitment to scientific research continue to serve as models for researchers and scientists everywhere.

Conclusively, In his personal life, he experienced a combination of intense academic pursuits, strong family ties, and ongoing health issues. His big family and his marriage to Emma Wedgwood gave him a kind and encouraging atmosphere that helped him persevere in his scientific pursuits. His strict daily schedule and methodical approach to work allowed him to make significant contributions to science despite his crippling health problems. His vast collection of work and the legacy he left behind are still relevant today, underscoring the significant influence of his life and ideals on how we see the natural world.

Chapter 3

Legacy and Influence of Charles Darwin

Foundations of Evolutionary Biology: His most major contribution to science is his theory of evolution by natural selection, stated in his classic book, "On the Origin of Species" (1859). This hypothesis offers a unifying framework for understanding the variety of life on Earth. His painstaking observations, experimentation, and the integration of existing information into a cohesive theory changed biology from a descriptive discipline into an explanatory one. His insights set the path for the present synthesis of evolutionary biology, merging genetics, paleontology, systematics, and other fields.

Selection and Adaptation by Nature: The knowledge of how organisms adapt to their surroundings was completely transformed by his theory that natural selection serves as the main process of evolution. The way scientists understand the origins of life and the mechanisms behind biological variety has been profoundly altered by this concept. According to his idea, beneficial features spread across populations over many generations, causing the emergence of new species.

Selection of Sexual Activities: He extended his theory to include sexual selection, the process by which certain qualities boost an individual's chances of mating and passing on their genes, in "The Descent of Man, and Selection about Sex" (1871). This idea clarified the development of features, like the intricate plumage of the peacock, that may not be favorable for survival but are advantageous for successful reproduction.

Evolution of Humans: He made a revolutionary contribution to human evolution theory. He challenged the widely held belief in human uniqueness by arguing that humans and other monkeys had a common progenitor. His theories influenced later studies on human origins, behavior, and psychology and established the discipline of anthropology.

Impact on Diverse Scientific Domains

Modern Synthesis and Genetics: His work established the foundation for the incorporation of genetics into evolutionary theory, even though he was ignorant of genes or the processes behind heredity. The contemporary synthesis resulted from the early 20th-century rediscovery of Gregor Mendel's work on inheritance in conjunction with his theories. Natural selection and genetics were brought together in this synthesis to provide a thorough framework for comprehending evolution.

Geology and Palaeontology: His theories had an impact on geology and paleontology, especially on the principles of gradualism and the long timescale necessary for evolutionary processes. Subsequent paleontological and geological research was influenced by his discoveries on the distribution of fossils and extant animals, which confirmed the theory of slow change over millions of years.

Biodiversity and Conservation: Significant effects of his work may also be seen in ecology and conservation biology. His understanding of the relationships between species and their surroundings contributed to the founding of the science of ecology. Since natural selection and adaptation guide methods for maintaining biodiversity and managing ecosystems, an understanding of these concepts is essential to conservation efforts.

Impact on Religion and Philosophy

Implications for Philosophy: Philosophical ramifications of his hypothesis of evolution by natural selection were profound. It refuted the teleological theory, which holds that life is intentionally designed, and offered a naturalistic account of life's variety in its place. Existentialism, humanism, and other philosophical systems that prioritize natural processes and human agency above supernatural intervention were impacted by this change.

Religious Discussion and Disagreement: The release of "On the Origin of Species" sparked a heated discussion among religious groups. His hypothesis was seen as at odds with the literal reading of the Bible, especially the Genesis creation myth. This prompted a reassessment of religious convictions and further conversations over the compatibility of science and religion. While some religious communities continued to reject evolutionary theory, others modified their views to make room for it.

Reinterpretations Theological: The idea of divine creation was called into question by theologians and religious experts as a result of his research. Many theologians have attempted to reconcile evolution science with faith, resulting in a variety of interpretations. The concept of theistic evolution first appeared, putting forward the theory that God created life on Earth using natural processes, including evolution.

Social and Cultural Impact

Public Perception and Education: His theories had a significant impact on scientific education and public opinion. Generations of students' understanding of the life sciences have been shaped by the integration of evolutionary theory into biology courses around the globe. Public discussions on evolution vs creationism, especially in the US, show how his contributions continue to influence society's perceptions of science and education.

Arts and Literature: He had an impact on literature and the arts in addition to science. His thoughts prompted poets, painters, and authors to investigate issues of the human condition, change, and adaptability. Literary works, like those by Thomas Hardy Alfred Lord Tennyson's poems and novels address Darwinian themes and add to the larger cultural conversation on evolution and human nature.

Thoughts on Society and Politics: Though somewhat contentious, his theory of evolution has a considerable impact on social and political philosophy. In the late 19th and early 20th centuries, social Darwinism—a misapplication of Darwinian concepts used to justify social injustice, competitiveness, and imperialism—came into being. Although he did not personally endorse these concepts, his work has been used to further several social and political objectives.

Individual Legacy and Acknowledgment

Recognitions and Tributes: He was awarded several accolades and recognitions for his contributions to science both during his lifetime and after his death. In 1853, the Royal Society awarded him the Royal Medal, and in 1864, the Copley Medal. His burial at Westminster Abbey in 1882 is evidence of his importance to both British and international scientific history.

Day of Darwin: His Day is observed on February 12, the day of his birth, to commemorate his contributions to science and to further scientific inquiry and teaching. Worldwide events and activities are held on this day to honor his significant contributions.

Awards and Institutions: His influence on research and education is honored by the namesake of many organizations, grants, and initiatives. His discoveries in the Galápagos Islands, where his theory of evolution originated, are the focus of study and conservation efforts carried out by the Charles Darwin Foundation, which was founded in 1959.

Ongoing Investigations and Evolutionary Research

Biology of Evolution: Current evolutionary biology study carries on his legacy. To investigate the mechanics of evolution, the genetic basis of adaptation, and the origins of biodiversity, scientists build on his seminal work. The field of paleontology, genetics, and molecular biology is constantly expanding and improving our knowledge of how evolution works.

Evolution of Humans: Fossils, genetics, and comparative anatomy are just a few of the tools used in the ongoing investigation of human evolution that reveals the intricate tale of our beginnings. His discoveries on the shared origin of primates and humans continue to be crucial to this subject, influencing research on the physiology, genetics, and behavior of humans.

Climate Variations and Protection: His theories on adaptation and the impact of the environment are essential for tackling modern issues like biodiversity loss and climate change. His work is still relevant today because conservation techniques increasingly depend on evolutionary concepts to manage and conserve species in changing habitats.

Conclusively, He left behind a rich and varied legacy that included important scientific advancements, deep implications for philosophy and religion, and a lasting impact on culture and society. In addition to revolutionizing biology, his idea of evolution by natural selection offered a cohesive framework for comprehending life on Earth. He is regarded as one of the most significant people in scientific history because his work continues to influence and guide scientific research, teaching, and public conversation. His dedication to exacting observation, thorough testing, and knowledge-seeking established a benchmark for scientific investigation that is still in place today.

Change in Perceptions Throughout the Beagle Voyage

The five-year HMS Beagle expedition (1831–1836) significantly altered his perspectives on religion and environment. He began to doubt the literal interpretation of the Bible, particularly the creation myth in Genesis, as a result of his observations of the variety of life, geological formations, and fossils. His perspective underwent a dramatic transformation when he saw that species were not unchangeable creations but may undergo change throughout time.

Natural History and Geology: Deep time and sluggish geological processes were concepts that Darwin first encountered via his study of geology, especially through the writings of Charles Lyell. The biblical chronology was in stark contrast to Lyell's uniformitarian assumptions, which held that the Earth's characteristics were formed by continuous processes over enormous periods. These concepts affected his comprehension of natural history and fueled his increasing doubts about conventional theological explanations.

Evolutionary Theory's Development and Its Effect on Faith

Building on the Theory: After his return to England, he worked on refining his theory of natural selection-based evolution. This procedure required a great deal of investigation, testing, and communication with other scientists. As his theories developed, he became aware that his hypothesis would contradict long-held religious doctrine on the genesis of life.

Progressive Loss of Traditional Views: In the next twenty years, his theological beliefs changed. Even while he never fully abandoned religion, his belief in conventional Christianity began to decline. He found it difficult to reconcile his scientific discoveries with the idea of an all-powerful, loving god. He became even more disenchanted with the concept of divine design as a result of the issue of pain and the seeming brutality of nature.

On the Origin of Species" publication: The connection between science and religion underwent a sea change when "On the Origin of Species" was published in 1859. He understood that there may be opposition from the public and religious leaders. Although human evolution was not specifically discussed in the text, it was evident that natural processes rather than supernatural intervention were responsible for the variety of life. This was a significant divergence from the dominant theological interpretations.

Family dynamics and personal struggles

The Faith of Emma Darwin: Emma Wedgwood Darwin was a devoted Unitarian who had strong religious beliefs. She was also his wife. Despite their differences in opinion, they had many passionate conversations and exchanged letters that demonstrated their profound regard for one another. Emma worried about her husband's spiritual health and the potential effects of his scientific work on his religion. Their communication reveals a deep inner battle to strike a balance between respect, affection, and opposing viewpoints.

Introspection and Individual Tragedies: When his beloved daughter Annie passed away in 1851, it had a significant impact on his religion. As he struggled with the anguish he saw in both his own life and the natural world, this tragedy deepened his doubts about a loving and righteous god. With Annie's passing, his views on religion began to diverge even more, as he struggled to make sense of her suffering in light of conventional wisdom.

Religious controversy and public perception

Acceptance of Darwin's Theories: "On the Origin of Species" sparked intense discussion and controversy when it was published. Even though his theory was widely accepted by scientists and intellectuals, institutions and religious leaders strongly opposed it. His theories, according to his detractors, damaged society's moral and spiritual underpinnings by casting doubt on the concepts of individual uniqueness and divine creation.

Supporters of Darwin: Several well-known people defended his theories against objections from religion. Known as "his Bulldog," Thomas Huxley was an ardent supporter who openly argued against opponents from religion and emphasized the scientific validity of evolution. American botanist and devoted Christian Asa Grey suggested that natural selection may be a tool used by God to make sense of his theories.

Affect on Religious Thought: Theologians and academics of religion were forced by his findings to reconsider how they interpreted the Bible and the coexistence of science and faith. The concept of theistic evolution arose, which suggested that God created life via evolutionary processes. This viewpoint made it possible for some religious people to embrace scientific answers without renouncing their beliefs.

The Later Years and Legacy of Darwin

Persistent Doubt: He remained a cautious agnostic into old age. Though he continued to respect religious ideas, he was not personally persuaded by conventional arguments for God's existence. He kept researching scientific issues and exchanging letters with both religious and nonreligious intellectuals.

Life Story and Thoughts: Towards the conclusion of his life, he wrote an autobiography in which he openly acknowledged his changing beliefs about religion. He acknowledged the boundaries of human comprehension while expressing a feeling of humility and doubt. Recognizing the intricacy of the issues surrounding existence and creation, he described himself as an agnostic rather than openly proclaiming himself to be an atheist.

Importance After Death: He passed away in 1882, yet his theories persisted in influencing both religious and scientific views. The argument between creationism and evolution remained, especially in educational settings. The continuous debate between the teaching of evolution in American schools and conservative Christian views was brought to light by the Scopes "Monkey" Trial at the beginning of the 20th century.

Contemporary Views: The connection between his ideas and religion is still complicated today. Many religious traditions have managed to incorporate evolutionary theory into their teachings, seeing no intrinsic contradiction between science and religion. For example, the Catholic Church upholds the spiritual and moral aspects of human life while acknowledging the validity of evolutionary biology.

Ongoing Discussions: Even with increased acceptance, discussions over creationism and evolution persist, especially among more conservative religious circles. The late 20th-century intelligent design movement makes the case for the presence of an intelligent creator based on the complexity of biological systems to refute Darwinian evolution.

Conclusively, Throughout his life, his connection with religion changed and became more nuanced. He wrestled with difficult issues regarding religion, science, and the natural world from his early religious upbringing and plans to become a clergyman, through the transformational journey aboard the Beagle, to the formulation and publishing of his theory of evolution by natural selection. He came to a respected agnosticism as a result of his difficulties with religious belief, which were affected by both personal tragedies and scientific discoveries. His theories caused a great deal of religious conflict, which led to new theological viewpoints and reevaluations of the Bible. His contributions to the conversation between science and religion have had a lasting influence on our understanding of the variety and beginnings of life.

Last Years and Demise

He struggled with several persistent health issues throughout his life, some of which proved especially crippling in his latter years. He had several symptoms, such as migraines, heart palpitations, extreme exhaustion, and significant stomach pain. Throughout his life, he saw several doctors, but no conclusive diagnosis was ever made. These days, researchers have conjectured that he may have suffered from irritable bowel syndrome (IBS), Crohn's illness, or Chagas disease.

He found a haven at Down House in Kent, where he could continue his scientific studies and take care of his health. He carefully planned his daily schedule to meet his medical requirements. When his energy was at its peak in the morning, he usually woke early and worked. He worked on his research and writing till early afternoon after taking a midmorning break. He would often take walks around his property in the afternoons, which provided him with exercise and a chance to observe the natural world. He read or played backgammon with his family in the evenings.

Research Projects and Articles

Ongoing Studies: He continued his scientific endeavors despite his persistent ailments. His final years were fruitful, during which he made important contributions to several academic disciplines. His large-scale research on plant biology produced works like "The Power of Movement in Plants" (1880) and "The Formation of Vegetable Mold through the Action of Worms" (1881). His lifelong interest and methodical dedication to scientific research were evident in these publications.

Interaction and Cooperation: He kept up a vast network of scientific communication, which was essential to his studies. He was able to exchange ideas, get information, and keep up with advancements across a range of scientific fields thanks to these letters. His partnerships with scientists like Asa Grey and Joseph Dalton Hooker gave his research important credibility and support.

Personal and Family Life

Family Assistance: In his final years, his family was a vital source of both practical and emotional support. Emma, his wife, supported him in his career and helped him manage his health. She was his constant companion and carer. Their offspring, particularly those who followed in the footsteps of Francis Darwin and became scientists, helped with his experiments and edited his publications.

Secular Misfortunes: He had personal catastrophes, such as the loss of three of his children, while coming from a close-knit family. The loss of his daughter, Anne Elizabeth ("Annie") Darwin, in 1851 was especially tragic and had a significant impact on his view on life and religious convictions. His mistrust of a loving god grew as a result of these personal setbacks, and he became even more at odds with conventional religious beliefs.

Public Acknowledgment and Debate

Acknowledgment from Science: The scientific world gave him a great deal of credit for his achievements. Among the many awards he received were the Copley Medal in 1864 and the Royal Medal from the Royal Society in 1853. These honors showed how highly his contemporaries regarded his work, despite his reclusive personality and health problems.

Public and Theological Discussion: The release of "On the Origin of Species" and other books provoked intense discussion and controversy, especially among religious communities.

Conventional beliefs about creation and human origins were called into question by the notion of evolution by natural selection. He was often hesitant to participate openly in public discussions, preferring to let others—like Thomas Huxley, dubbed "his Bulldog"—argue his position. He did, however, pay careful attention to the conversations and worry about how his work might affect society and religion.

Enduring Years and Heritage

Persistent Health Reduction: His condition worsened over the latter years of his life. He had frequent episodes of sickness that often left him bedridden for protracted periods. He continued to be a thinker despite these obstacles, working on his scientific publications and communicating with other scientists.

Death: At the age of 73, he passed away on April 19, 1882. His long-standing health problems were exacerbated by heart disease, which was the cause of his death. He spent his last days at Down House with his family, who took care of him and supported him. With his death, a great life devoted to intellectual and scientific pursuits came to an end.

Honors and Burial: His important honor, which recognized his contributions to science and society, was to be buried at Westminster Abbey. Numerous well-known people from the public and scientific domains attended his burial, underscoring the broad regard and esteem he had earned over his career. The fact that he was buried beside other great scientists and historical personalities demonstrated the long-lasting influence of his work.

After-death Impact: Modern evolutionary biology is based on his hypothesis of evolution by natural selection. Darwinian evolution and Mendelian genetics were combined in the early 20th century to create the modern synthesis, which offered a thorough framework for comprehending the mechanics of evolution. This synthesis strengthened Darwin's reputation as a founding figure in biology by elaborating and improving his theories.

Impact on Diverse Scientific Fields: Beyond biology, his discoveries had a significant influence on many other scientific fields. His theories shaped study goals and approaches in disciplines like ecology, paleontology, anthropology, and geology. knowledge of the dynamics of natural systems and the evolution of life on Earth has become dependent on a knowledge of natural selection and adaptation.

Legacy of Culture and Philosophy: Beyond science, his theories impacted philosophical and cultural views. His writings questioned conventional wisdom on humanity's role in the natural world, leading to reconsiderations of existential, ethical, and theological issues. In addition to sparking discussions on morality, the purpose of life, and human nature, the idea of evolution by natural selection has had a significant role in wider intellectual and cultural movements.

Impact on Education: His contributions to science have influenced schooling for a long time. Global biology courses include evolutionary theory as a basic component, which shapes students' understanding of the life sciences for generations. His contributions continue to stimulate a greater understanding of the variety and complexity of life in students, educators, and researchers.

Popular and Public Culture: The influence of him may also be seen in popular culture. Numerous books, documentaries, films, and creative works have been inspired by his life and work. His visage, often shown with his characteristic beard and reflective look, has come to represent scientific research and intellectual curiosity.

Conclusively, The latter years of his life were characterized by both personal struggles and professional successes. He continued to be a committed scientist and made substantial contributions to many different disciplines of research while having long-term health concerns. His extraordinary life devoted to comprehending the natural world came to an end with his death in 1882. He left behind a lasting legacy that includes his revolutionary theory of evolution by natural selection and its significant influence on philosophy, science, and society. His research continues to be a pillar of contemporary biology and a shining example of the value of scientific investigation and intellectual curiosity.

Darwin in the Modern Era

The foundation of contemporary evolutionary biology continues to be his idea of evolution by natural selection. His discoveries paved the way for our current knowledge of the mechanisms behind Earth's biodiversity. Extensive data from a variety of domains, including molecular biology, ecology, genetics, and paleontology, now supports the notion. The modern synthesis, which brought together Darwinian theory and Mendelian genetics in the early 1900s, strengthened the theory of evolution even further. Strong evidence supporting his hypothesis has been offered by developments in genomics and molecular biology. The genetic similarities and differences supporting evolutionary links have been made visible by the sequencing of genomes from a diverse variety of creatures. By using methods like molecular phylogenetics and comparative genomics, scientists may track the evolutionary history of each species and validate his postulated patterns of descent with modification.

There is still strong evidence for evolution in the fossil record. Findings of transitional fossils, such as those that connect fish to tetrapods or dinosaurs to birds, show the slow transitions that take place over millions of years. These results provide credence to his gradualist theory, which holds that significant evolutionary shifts emerge from the accumulation of little, gradual movements. Fundamental concepts in ecology and conservation biology are those of him on natural selection and adaptability. Conservation efforts are informed by our understanding of how species adapt to their habitats, especially in light of climate change and habitat degradation. Darwinian theory is the foundation for ideas like species interactions, ecological niches, and adaptive radiation.

Modern Evolutionary Theory Developments and Challenges

Developmental Synthesis Extended: An extended evolutionary synthesis (EES) has been proposed as a result of recent advances in evolutionary biology. Although it draws on Darwinian principles, this framework also integrates recent discoveries and ideas from disciplines including developmental biology, ecology, and epigenetics. The EES places a strong emphasis on how developmental processes, ecological interactions, and non-genetic inheritance shape the course of evolution. The EES aims to give a more thorough knowledge of evolutionary processes, without superseding his theory.

Evolution of Humans and Anthropology: The intricate past of our species is still being uncovered by research on the evolution of humans. The complex web of relationships between various hominin species and the environmental factors that influenced human evolution has been made clear by developments in paleoanthropology, archaeology, and genetics. These findings have greatly broadened his initial idea of human evolution and contributed to a better comprehension of our ancestry and adaptability.

Medicine in Evolution: Evolutionary medicine is the expanding discipline of applying evolutionary ideas to medicine. It aims to comprehend how evolutionary processes affect both health and illness. The idea of evolutionary incompatibilities, for instance, clarifies how characteristics that were beneficial in ancient settings might be a factor in contemporary health issues. Strategies for fighting illnesses are also informed by knowledge of the evolutionary history of infections and human immune responses.

Intelligent Design and Biotechnology: His theories on artificial and natural selection have a significant impact on biotechnology. The concepts of variation and selection are used in genetic engineering, synthetic biology, and selective breeding. Darwinian theory's practical applications are shown by these technologies, which make it possible to produce new industrial uses, medications, and crops.

The Legacy of Darwin in the 21st Century

International Scientific Significance: The continuous studies and discoveries made by the international scientific community are clear examples of his legacy. His theory of evolution via natural selection still serves as a foundation for and a direction for scientific research in many other fields. Evolutionary biology conferences, research centers, and academic programs make sure that his legacy lives on in science teaching and research.

Social and Cultural Influence: His theories have influenced cultural and societal conceptions of nature, humans, and our role in the universe. Our view of human identity, ethics, and the interconnection of all life is both challenged and enhanced by the notion of evolution. Darwinian themes are still relevant to public personalities, authors, and artists, demonstrating the broad influence of his work on modern culture.

Climatic and Ecological Initiatives: In light of the current global environmental issues, his observations about the interdependence of species and their habitats are becoming more and more pertinent. Evolutionary concepts are often used in conservation efforts to preserve biodiversity and maintain sustainable ecosystem management. To solve concerns like climate change, habitat loss, and species extinction, it is essential to comprehend the evolutionary history and adaptive capability of species.

Public Acknowledgment and Tributary: His accomplishments are widely acknowledged and honored in several ways. His legacy is honored and public participation in science is encouraged via institutions, prizes, and events that carry his name. Celebrated worldwide on February 12, Darwin Day honors his accomplishments and promotes scientific knowledge.

Conclusively, His legacy continues to have a significant impact on modern science, philosophy, culture, and society in several ways. His theory of natural selection-based evolution still serves as a fundamental framework for comprehending biological variety and the mechanisms behind biological change. Darwinian concepts have been elaborated upon and strengthened by advances in paleontology, genetics, molecular biology, and other sciences, demonstrating the ongoing importance of these ideas. Beyond science, Darwin's influence may be seen in how he shaped popular perception of nature, education, religious discussions, and philosophical conversation. His theories upend conventional wisdom, stimulate fresh lines of investigation, and provide guidance for real-world uses in biotechnology, medicine, and conservation. His legacy stands as a tribute to the strength of scientific inquiry and the pursuit of knowledge as we continue to investigate and comprehend the intricacies of life.

The Memorandum That Transformed History:

He received Wallace's article in June 1858, which presented the theory of natural selection in a way that was almost exact to his own. Fearing Wallace would get all the credit for a theory he had been working on for more than twenty years, he was astonished and upset.

Lyell and Hooker's Role: His close friends, the botanist Joseph Dalton Hooker and the geologist Charles Lyell, also read Wallace's article. Wallace's study was acknowledged as significant, and his unpublished research was given precedence. Lyell and Hooker suggested a combined presentation to the Linnean Society of London to guarantee that both men were given credit.

The Presentation to the Linnean Society: Lyell and Hooker delivered Wallace's article and his unpublished passages to the Linnean Society on July 1, 1858. Among the items in the presentation were:

- A letter describing his theories to Asa Grey in 1857.
- A synopsis of his natural selection article from 1844.
- Wallace's natural selection essay.

The members of the society did not immediately understand the importance of the new idea, which contributed to the mediocre reception of the presentation.

Publishing and Working Together

On the Origin of Species: He was inspired to act after the combined presentation. His massive body of study was distilled into a single book, "On the Origin of Species," which was released in November 1859. The book established his dominance in the area of biology by outlining the evidence for natural selection and turning it into a fundamental work.

Wallace's Reaction: With grace and awe, Wallace—who remained in the Malay Archipelago—heard of the combined presentation and his later publication. He showed no signs of bitterness, acknowledging his importance and the important foundation he had set. Wallace's books "On the Law Which Have Regulated the Introduction of New Species" (1855) and "The Malay Archipelago" (1869) furthered his contributions to the idea.

Eternal Companionship and Respect for One Another

Continuous Communication: During their lifetimes, him and Wallace had cordial and courteous contact. They discussed a broad variety of scientific subjects in their letters, such as human evolution, biogeography, and natural selection. Wallace recognized his intellectual debt to him and often sought his assistance.

Diversities of Opinions: Him and Wallace respected one another, yet they did not have the same opinions.

Sexual Selection: To explain features that seemed to be favorable for mating but detrimental to survival, he postulated the idea of sexual selection. Wallace was dubious and thought that natural selection was the main cause of these features.

Human Evolution: According to him, sexual and natural selection processes completely apply to humans. Wallace, on the other hand, thought that our moral and intellectual capacities were too developed to be fully explained by these processes and proposed a higher power or spiritual influence.

Teamwork Is Key: The two guys worked together on several scientific projects. For example, Wallace defended and clarified his beliefs in "Darwinism" (1889), reaffirming their mutual goal of expanding our knowledge of evolution.

Identification and Heritage

Honors & Awards: Throughout their lives, him and Wallace were bestowed with a multitude of honors:

Darwin: Awarded the Copley and Royal Medals, elected as a Fellow of the Royal Society, and buried at Westminster Abbey.

Wallace: Received the Darwin Medal, the Order of Merit, and the Royal Society's Royal Medal. In 1908, Wallace was also awarded the Darwin-Wallace Medal by the Linnean Society in remembrance of their joint presentation's 50th anniversary.

Science-related Influence: It is impossible to overestimate him and Wallace's contributions to evolutionary biology. Their joint efforts and individual discoveries established the groundwork for contemporary biology. Their beliefs were further supported by the 20th-century "modern synthesis," which combined their concepts with genetics.

Tributaries: The scientific community still pays tribute to these two guys. The Linnean Society bestows the Darwin-Wallace Medal to honor exceptional contributions to the field of evolutionary biology. Their legacy is honored and further study in the subject of evolution is encouraged by institutions, prizes, and events bearing their names.

Conclusively, The partnership in scientific discovery is shown by the interaction between him and Alfred Russel Wallace. Their separate but concurrent advancement of the theory of evolution by natural selection is a prime example of how brilliant brains may come up with ground-breaking concepts. One of the most significant scientific ideas in history was established thanks to their cooperation, respect for one another, and communication. The fact that him and Wallace's contributions to science are still relevant today highlights how their legacy inspires and informs the study of evolution.

Chapter 4

Memories and Biographies of Family

His life and contributions have been well chronicled, not only by his works but also by the memoirs and biographies written by his relatives. These first-hand narratives provide distinctive insights into his personality, way of life, and the close-knit family dynamics that encouraged his scientific pursuits. The personal memories of his wife and children, the contributions of his family to his biographies, and the influence of these works on our comprehension of his life and legacy will all be covered in this investigation.

Emma Darwin: A Chronicler and Lifelong Companion

De Darwin, Emma Wedgwood: His first cousin and wife, Emma Wedgwood, was very important to both his personal and professional lives. His scientific skepticism was balanced by Emma, a well-educated, intellectual, and devoutly religious woman born into the wealthy Wedgwood family. After being married in 1839, Emma became a committed mother to their ten children and an essential collaborator in his career.

Copies and Individual Memories: The letters and autobiographies of Emma Darwin provide insightful accounts of his day-to-day activities and his battles with long-term sickness. Her letters shed light on her roles as a moral supporter, collaborator in thought, and carer. He was able to work in a stable and peaceful environment at Down House because of Emma's thorough management of the household. Her memories, which have been kept in family archives, show her great regard and love for her husband as well as the difficulties they overcame together.

Corrected Letters and Memories from the Family:
Many of his letters were edited and archived by Emma after his death, and they were eventually published, giving academics a close-up look at his ideas and private life. Beyond his scientific accomplishments, his human side has been shown via these letters and Emma's remarks and notes.

A Family of Biographers: The Contributions of the Children

Darwin, Francis: The third son of Charles and Emma Darwin, Francis, was a botanist who made substantial contributions to the documentation and promotion of his father's work. The most famous book of Darwin's autobiographical notes and letters, "The Life and Letters of Charles Darwin" (1887), contains recollections of the author's family as well as personal tales. Francis edited numerous volumes of these notes. This book, which offers background information and analysis of his life experiences as well as his scientific accomplishments, is still the key resource for learning about him.

"Life and Letters of Charles Darwin": "The Life and Letters of Charles Darwin" is a comprehensive collection of family members' comments, autobiographical bits, and his letters that was published in three volumes. The first book concentrates on his upbringing, schooling, and HMS Beagle expedition. His latter scientific achievements, personal life, and connections with contemporaries are covered in the second and third volumes. Francis's editing notes and comments emphasize his intellectual growth and difficulties while offering insightful background and interpretation.

Memories of Other Children: His memory was also preserved by a number of his other offspring. Henrietta, his daughter, assisted in organizing and editing his letters, for example. Another son, Leonard Darwin, wrote about his father's impact on society and science. The children of him worked together to ensure that their father's life and contributions were presented in a thorough and varied manner.

Grandkids and Upcoming Generations

Barlow, Nora: His granddaughter Nora Barlow, who was the son of his son Sir George Darwin, was another important biographer. She oversaw the editing and publication of "The Autobiography of Charles Darwin 1809-1882," which had previously unpublished sections that offered more frank insights into his personal and religious convictions. Barlow's research offered a more comprehensive and nuanced view of his inner ideas and philosophical reflections.

Darwin, His Children and His Other Legacy : In 2012, his great-great-grandson Randal Keynes wrote a biography titled "Darwin and His Children.

His Other Legacy." It explores the fatherhood and connections Darwin had with his children, as well as the family elements of his life. Keynes's work emphasizes the loving and supportive atmosphere that he fostered, which had a big influence on the lives and careers of his kids.

Personal Life and Family Dynamics

Down House Day-to-Day: His family members' memoirs and recollections provide a vivid picture of everyday life at Down House. These narratives highlight his regimented daily schedule, his commitment to scientific inquiry, and the private family moments that interspersed his workday. Everyday hikes, scholarly talks, and nights spent reading or playing games were all part of the Darwin family's routine. These particulars deepen our comprehension of him as a committed spouse and parent in addition to his role as a scientist.

Well-being and Health: Recollections from the family often highlight his continuous health issues. His life and career were significantly impacted by his chronic disease, and his family's support was essential to helping him manage his symptoms. He was able to continue his studies despite health issues thanks in large part to Emma Darwin's attentive care and the kids' awareness of their father's demands.

Emotional and Intellectual Assistance: He received mental and emotional assistance in addition to physical care from his family. Emma had intelligent conversations with him and supported his scientific endeavors, even though she was a devout Christian. Many of his children went on to become scientists, and they often helped their father with his research and writing. Within the household, this intellectual atmosphere promoted scientific curiosity and innovation.

Impact on Scholarship on Darwin

Main References for Scholars: Researchers examining his life and work might get original materials from his biographies and family memories. These records provide first-hand information and intimate insights that are priceless for historical and biographical studies. They put his scientific accomplishments in perspective and illuminate the life events that influenced his beliefs.

Making the Scientist Human: Family stories help to humanize him by showing him as a devoted parent, friend, and spouse rather than merely as an impersonal scientific entity. Readers and academics may better understand the nuances of his character and the interactions between his personal and professional lives thanks to this first-hand account. Gaining insight into his personal struggles and family ties enhances our understanding of his contributions to science and gives his image more dimension.

Impact on Contemporary Biographies: Subsequent historians and biographers have drawn inspiration from in-depth family memoirs and biographies. Drawing heavily on these original materials, contemporary books on him often expand upon the groundwork established by his family. His legacy is safeguarded and continuously reevaluated in light of fresh findings and viewpoints because of this continuity.

Conclusively, His life is presented in a rich and complex manner via family stories and biographies, which highlight the interpersonal connections and experiences that shaped his scientific breakthroughs. A detailed and personal portrayal of him has been preserved because of the efforts of his wife, Emma, his children, and subsequent generations. These narratives provide light on the significance of familial support for his research and provide insightful perspectives on the man who developed the theory of evolution. These family manuscripts, which are sources, are still crucial for comprehending his legacy and guaranteeing that his scientific accomplishments and life narrative are honored.

The variety of films and books that Charles Darwin produced or acted in

One of the most important scientists in history, he has been the focus of several novels and motion pictures. Each of these works—which vary from dramatizations to speculative fiction to biographical narratives—offers a distinctive viewpoint on the man, his contributions, and his legacy. This investigation will focus on important he-related films and publications, emphasizing how they depict the man, his scientific achievements, and the significance of his ideas.

1.) Charles Darwin in Films (2009) Creation

Overview: "Creation," a biographical play directed by Jon Amiel, is based on the book "Annie's Box" written by Randal Keynes, his great-great-grandson. In the movie, Jennifer Connelly plays Emma Darwin, while Paul Bettany plays him.

Plot: The film focuses on his battle to write "On the Origin of Species' ' while dealing with Annie's death. It delves into the mental and emotional struggles he had, as well as how his ideas affected his devout Catholic wife Emma.

Portrayal: "Creation" depicts him as a pitiful and kind man, divided between his sorrow and his scientific findings. The personal details of his family life and the significant obstacles he faced are shown in the film, which also emphasizes his loving but tense relationship with his wife.

2.) "The Darwin Adventure" released in 1972

Overview: Nicholas Clay plays him in the Jack Couffer-directed film "The Darwin Adventure". His journey on the HMS Beagle is the main subject of this British biographical movie.

Plot: The movie tells the story of his travels, highlighting the observations and findings that helped him come up with his theory of evolution. It illustrates the key events and new scientific discoveries discovered along the journey.

Portrayal: Darwin is seen in the movie as a young naturalist who is driven and curious. It highlights his attention to detail and how his journey changed the way he thought about science.

3.) Darwin's Darkest Hour (2009)

Overview: A two-hour National Geographic and Nova television documentary featuring Frances

O'Connor as Emma Darwin and Henry Ian Cusick as him.

Plot: The documentary focuses on the crucial year of 1858 when Alfred Russel Wallace's article on natural selection was sent to him. It draws attention to his family's emotional support as well as the pressure he faced to publish his work.

Portrayal: He is seen in the movie as a troubled scientist who is worried about how his contentious theories will be received. It explores his personal and professional life, highlighting the mental and emotional upheaval he went through.

4.) The 2009 film "The Voyage That Shook the World"

Overview: A dramatized account of his life and travels, presented in the guise of a documentary produced by Creation Ministries International.

Plot: Following his journey aboard the HMS Beagle, the movie follows the evolution of his theory of evolution. Interviews with scientists and historians are included, offering a critical analysis of his contributions.

Portrayal: By challenging the ramifications of his ideas and recognizing his accomplishments, the movie seeks to provide a fair and impartial perspective. It examines his theories' wider effects on science and society, presenting him as a trailblazing but contentious figure.

Books with Charles Darwin in Them

The following explains the numerous books in which Charles Darwin has co-authored;

Life Stories: Janet Browne's two-volume biography, "Charles Darwin: Voyaging" and "Charles Darwin, the Power of Place," is usually considered to be the only accurate account of his life. From his early years and the Beagle expedition to the publication of "On the Origin of Species" and his subsequent work, Browne's painstaking research and compelling narrative provide an in-depth examination of his personal and professional path.

Adrian Desmond and James Moore's "Darwin: The Life of a Tormented Evolutionist, this thorough biography explores the intricacies of his personality, his scientific accomplishments, and the social and religious obstacles he encountered. He is shown in great detail by Desmond and Moore, who highlight both his successes and hardships.

Works of Fiction: Harry Thompson's historical fiction "This Thing of Darkness" dramatizes the connection between him and the HMS Beagle's commander, Robert FitzRoy. The book tells the story of his journey and the discussions that influenced his theory of evolution in a way that is both instructive and fictionalized.

Mrs. Darwin's Garden" **by** *Diana Souhami:* This book tells a fictionalized story of Emma Darwin's life with him, with an emphasis on Emma. It delves into her viewpoint on his work and their family life, offering a unique insight into the individual effects of his scientific pursuits.

Well-Known Science Books: David Quammen's book "The Reluctant Mr. Darwin" offers a narrative history of his life and the evolution of his theory, with a focus on the time following his return from the Beagle trip. A wider readership can understand the intricate scientific concepts because of Quammen's captivating writing style.

Darwin's Ghost: The Origin of Species Updated" by Steve Jones: Jones adapts his "On the Origin of Species" to reflect contemporary scientific findings. The goal of the book is to show how his theories are still relevant today by bridging the gap between his earlier research and modern evolutionary biology.

Films for Education and Documentaries, The 2009 book "Charles Darwin and the Tree of Life"

Overview: David Attenborough hosts a BBC program commemorating the 200th anniversary of Charles Darwin's birth and the 150th anniversary of "On the Origin of Species."

Content: The film delves into his biography, his journey aboard the Beagle, and the growth of his theory of evolution. Attenborough looks at the data in favor of natural selection as well as the influence of his theories on contemporary science.

Portrayal: Darwin is shown in the movie as a revolutionary theorist whose discoveries revolutionized our knowledge of life on Earth. His contributions are emphasized both historically and scientifically in Attenborough's narration.

Darwin's Struggle: The Evolution of the Origin of Species" (2009)

Overview: A 20-year era in which he developed his theory of natural selection is the subject of this BBC program.

Content: Featuring dramatized portions and interviews with scientists and historians, the documentary explores the intellectual, emotional, and societal obstacles Darwin encountered while working on "On the Origin of Species.

Portrayal: The movie emphasizes his tenacity and commitment, showing him as a careful scientist motivated by curiosity and a search for knowledge.

Importance and Implications

Depiction of Darwin's Personality: A variety of publications and films about Charles Darwin provide a complex portrait of the man. These pieces provide a variety of viewpoints on the man who developed the theory of evolution, from his work as a trailblazing scientist to his personal hardships and family life. While dramatized and fictionalized stories focus on the interpersonal and emotional elements of his life, biographies and films often highlight his academic rigor and tenacity.

Comprehending Evolutionary Theory's Development: The development of evolutionary theory is also better-understood thanks to these videos and publications. They draw attention to the scientific, social, and religious milieu in which he operated, highlighting the difficulties he had in disseminating his theories worldwide. These texts emphasize his importance to science by tracing his painstaking investigation and the progressive elaboration of his hypothesis.

Impact on Education and Culture: His image in literature and movies has influenced education and culture greatly. A wider audience may understand complicated scientific ideas via documentaries and popular science publications, which increases appreciation for his contributions. Historical narratives that are intriguing and emphasize the human aspect of scientific discovery captivate readers and viewers, bringing history to life via dramatized reports and novels.

Persistent Legacy: The continued interest in his life and work is evidence of his lasting legacy. His contributions to science will always be acknowledged and appreciated thanks to the great variety of films and books that have been produced. His influence on our comprehension of the natural world is still evident in these depictions, stimulating inquiry, discussion, and wonder.

In Conclusion, Many novels and films have been written on his life and career, and each one offers a different perspective on his personality and scientific accomplishments. These works, which range from in-depth biographies and instructional documentaries to dramatized films and fictionalized narratives, add to a thorough and complex knowledge of his legacy. They draw attention to the difficulties he encountered in his personal and professional life, the evolution of his ground-breaking theory, and the lasting impact of his contributions to society and science. His narrative is still inspiring and educating people thanks to these depictions, which guarantees that his legacy will always be an important part of our scientific and cultural history.

How the story of Charles Darwin teaches moral and practical truths.

There are many ethical and practical lessons to be learned from his life and work that go far beyond scientific boundaries. His path from an inquisitive child naturalist to one of history's most significant men is replete with lessons about tenacity, modesty, intellectual curiosity, and the guts to defy expectations. This in-depth analysis will examine the moral and life lessons that his story imparts, demonstrating how his experiences and accomplishments may serve as an inspiration and guidance for others in a variety of spheres of life.

1. The Value of Inquisitiveness and Lifelong Learning

Initial Inquiry and Discovery: He showed an unquenchable interest in the natural world from an early age. His early fascination with gathering specimens and studying the natural world served as the basis for his later scientific pursuits. This characteristic emphasizes how important it is to foster curiosity and a love of learning from a young age.

Unwavering Devotion to Knowledge: His enthusiasm for learning did not decrease with age. His studies years after the HMS Beagle voyage demonstrate his unwavering commitment to deepening his knowledge of nature. This lesson emphasizes how important it is to always learn new things and develop intellectually throughout life.

2. tenacity in the face of difficulty

Personal Struggles with Chronic Illness: His life was characterized by persistent health problems that resulted in severe mental and physical suffering. He continued to stay committed to his job despite these obstacles, often carrying out experiments and writing while confined to bed. His tenacity in the face of difficulty serves as an example of the importance of resiliency and willpower.

Rejection and Scientific Obstacles: When he first proposed his hypothesis of evolution by natural selection, both the scientific community and the general public were skeptical and opposed. He highlights the value of tenacity and sticking to one's principles by his determination to keep going despite the challenges to improve and defend his ideals.

3. The Bravery to Question Accepted Norms

Contesting Establishing Theories: The ideas that were widely held at the time, especially the literal interpretation of the creation myth found in the Bible and the idea that species are immutable, were profoundly challenged by his study. His willingness to confront and question accepted wisdom emphasizes the need for critical thinking and intellectual fearlessness.

Effect on Society and Science: The 1859 release of "On the Origin of Species" provoked intense discussion and ultimately resulted in a paradigm change in the scientific understanding of life. His courage to put out contentious ideas serves as an example of the revolutionary power that may result from daring to confront the established quo.

4. Being humble and receptive to new ideas

Recognising Other People's Contributions: He was kind in his appreciation of the contributions made by his peers, like Alfred Russel Wallace, whose own development of the idea of natural selection paralleled his own. These qualities of humility and willingness to work together are essential in every line of work.

Teaching Theories and Refinement: He embodies intellectual humility in his readiness to modify and improve his views in light of fresh information. He acknowledged that scientific knowledge is always changing and remained receptive to criticism and new information. This lesson emphasizes how important it is to be adaptable and willing to change one's mind.

5. The Function of Support Systems and Families

Emma Darwin's Assistance: Emma, his wife, was an important person in his life since she supported him both intellectually and emotionally. Her religious convictions notwithstanding, she appreciated and encouraged his scientific endeavors. This facet of his life serves as a reminder of how crucial family and friends can be in helping one attain both personal and professional objectives.

The Intellectual Environment of the Family: His children often helped with his experiments and participated in scientific debates, making his home a center of intellectual activity. His family's caring and intellectually stimulating atmosphere emphasizes how important it is to have a loving and stimulating home life.

6. A Look Into Ethical Issues in Scientific Research

Benefit to Society: He was very aware of how his research might affect society, especially in light of the possibility that it would contradict moral and religious convictions. His thoughtful analysis of these effects serves as an example of the moral obligation that accompanies scientific advancement and discovery.

Honoring the Environment: His ardent reverence for the natural world and his thorough recording of its marvels demonstrate a moral approach to scientific inquiry. His work promotes a sustainable and moral relationship with nature by fostering a feeling of stewardship and responsibility towards the environment.

7. The Importance of Communication and Documentation

Careful Documentation: He kept thorough records of his observations, experiments, and thinking processes in his extensive diaries, notes, and letters. This painstaking documentation emphasizes how crucial it is to maintain complete records in any line of work to guarantee that information is appropriately transmitted and maintained.

Efficient Exchange of Concepts: His works, especially "On the Origin of Species," are characterized by their accessibility and clarity, which highlights the need for proficient communication in the exchange of complex concepts. His capacity to explain his ideas in a way that both scientists and the general public could grasp emphasizes how important it is to communicate engagingly and transparently.

8. Integrity and Intellectual Honesty

Taking Ownership of Uncertainty: He was open about the constraints and uncertainties surrounding his research. He was honest about the things he didn't know and the unsolved questions. In every industry where there is a need for credibility and trust, intellectual honesty and integrity are essential.

Dedication to Veracity: His a great example of integrity because of his unrelenting dedication to finding and revealing the truth, despite social and personal obstacles. His commitment to honesty and integrity in science serves as a vital example of ethical behavior.

9. The Life's Interdependence

Comprehending Evolutionary Connections: His explanation of how evolution demonstrates how all life is interrelated is among his greatest achievements. This insight promotes a more sympathetic and comprehensive understanding of the natural world by fostering a feeling of oneness and similarity among all living things.

Impact from a Human Viewpoint: His theories have radically changed how we think about how we fit into the natural world. His discovery of the common ancestry of all species has prompted a more linked and modest view of humanity's place in the larger scheme of things regarding other living forms.

10. History and Significance

Motivating Next Generations: In all academic fields, scientists, researchers, and intellectuals are still motivated by his life and contributions. His legacy is evidence of the lasting power of inquisitiveness, tenacity, and intellectual bravery. Future generations may use the teachings from his story as a guide to pursue knowledge and the truth.

Expanding Our Views: The scope of scientific investigation and comprehension has expanded due to the extensive consequences of his ideas. His work serves as a reminder of the value of expanding human knowledge and the enormous possibilities for discovery.

Conclusively, His life story is full of moral and life lessons that go beyond his revolutionary contributions to science. His boundless curiosity, fortitude in the face of difficulty, intellectual modesty, and ethical concerns are a great source of motivation and direction. His tale emphasizes the need for lifelong learning, critical thinking, and the guts to defy accepted wisdom. It emphasizes the need for good communication, family support, and the interconnection of all things. Above all, his unshakable dedication to honesty and truth stands as a timeless example of moral behavior and intellectual integrity. His legacy lives on via these teachings, providing insightful guidance for people from many backgrounds.

www.ingramcontent.com/pod-product-compliance
Lightning Source LLC
Chambersburg PA
CBHW071927210526
45479CB00002B/585